Reckless

The Outrageous
Lives of Nine
Kick-Ass Women

Gloria Mattioni

SEAL PRESS

Reckless
The Outrageous Lives of Nine Kick-Ass Women

Published by
Seal Press
An Imprint of Avalon Publishing Group, Incorporated
1400 65th Street, Suite 250
Emeryville, CA 94608

AVALON
publishing group incorporated

ISBN-10: 1-58005-148-0
ISBN-13: 978-1-58005-148-4

9 8 7 6 5 4 3 2 1

Library of Congress Cataloging-in-Publication Data

Mattioni, Gloria, 1957- Reckless : the outrageous lives of nine
kick-ass women / by Gloria Mattioni.

p. cm.

ISBN 1-58005-148-0

1. Women—United States—Biography. I. Title.

HQ1410.M39 2005

305.4'0973—dc22

2005014840

Cover and interior design by Domini Dragoone
Printed in the Canada by Transcontinental
Distributed by Publishers Group West

To my mother, Lalla Germani

Thanks to her, I've grown into a strong woman. She
has been a role model of independence, determination,
and free spirit. She never stopped fighting, and she
taught me to never give up.

No matter how ill, old, or fragile you may feel, Mom,
you'll always been my lioness and my warrior queen.

Contents

✦ ✦ ✦

Dreaming is the ability not only to point your finger at the moon, but to hitchhike all the way up there.

Introduction

WILD WOMEN

Did you see *Kill Bill* (either one) and enjoy it like a five-year-old dipping her fingers in a Nutella jar? Have you ever felt, deep in your gut, that God might just be a woman for imagining and giving life to the firecracker of a creation that is our world? Did you ever doubt that the seed of passion for adventure and exploration could be inscribed on a chromosome, and that these qualities are equally strong in both men and women? If you answered yes to at least one of the above questions, you've picked up the right book. I am going to introduce you to a series of women who are creative seekers and daredevils, reckless with the rules of conformity that they outright reject. They don't take no for an answer, and they don't settle on the cheapest way out. They take risks. They explore. They live life to its fullest. They represent everywoman, all the creative feminine force that comes together in a woman who is free to do as she chooses.

This is not to leave men out of the picture completely; I enjoy the company of all adventurous characters, no matter what gender disguise they come in. Yet there are so many books that show the male side of this same story that I decided to forge my own path and tell the stories of women I met over the years who answered the call of the wild. Long ago I committed myself to looking for them, even if I had to track them down on the icy Alaskan tundra, as I did with Libby Riddles, the first female winner of the Iditarod race across Alaska. Even if I have to cross plains, board airplanes and boats, and travel extreme distances, once I decide I need to meet a woman who has piqued my curiosity, I know no limits. I welcome the revelation of women's spirit and energy when presented to me as an unwrapped, simple gift. Recently, I got a gift in the form of a blog by my friend Heather, in which she describes her reason to impersonate Æon Flux at a Halloween Party:

> *Since the first time I saw her eyelash trapping*
> *the fly on MTV as a teenager, I was transfixed. She*
> *carried a gun. She killed men. (She killed women.)*
> *She wore barely anything. She worked for no one. She*
> *had control. She was out of control. She died.*
> *And she returned. She had the most fabulous hair*
> *I had ever seen. (Princess Leia couldn't even*
> *think about competing with Æon.) I wanted to be her*
> *then. Fifteen years ago as a teenage girl. I dreamt.*
> *I would be ass kicking, gun wielding, whip snapping,*
> *tongue probing, exotic, erotic, hardcore, soft worn,*
> *forever changing, never tied down. Constantly dying,*
> *always living.*
> —www.heathervescent.com

Reckless

If you recognize your own dreams in her words, then you'll enjoy meeting the women in this book. You can flip through the pages as you would with a photo album. Let their lives inspire you. Dance with Libby, Angelika, Barbara, Gevin, Julia, Lisa, Polly, Wilma, and Annie. Maybe you are one of the many outstanding women I haven't met yet. And maybe their stories will allow you to access parts of yourself that you are just beginning to uncover. I've dedicated years to seeking out a particular kind of woman, always faithful to my own conviction that life must be treated as a great adventure. No point in living it just to get by.

As long as I can remember, I've been allergic to routine. I have longed to explore and discover since my childhood. My feeling, and later my experience, told me that I wasn't the only girl to think and feel this way. I was more rebellious than others, less capable of settling down into an ordinary life. But as I got older, I realized that that longing for adventure is there in many women's minds, even when it's not acted upon.

I knew it was true because I grew up surrounded by women. I was born into a household of women in Milano, Italy. My dad was already gone by the time I was born, living a new life with another woman. My mother raised my older sister and me with the help of a sixteen-year-old babysitter. My mother worked long hours to provide us with opportunities other than just food on the table. Once a year she would pack us, the babysitter, and a ton of luggage into her 600 Fiat compact, and we would leave for a big adventure. Often this simply entailed crossing the border into Switzerland or France. The excitement, however, was as intense as if we had been taking a trip to the Caribbean.

This was my mom's idea of being successful: being able to provide her daughters with excitement, adventure, and exploration. We spent the rest of our summers with my paternal grandparents in a big country house in Laveno, a town

Introduction

on the shore of Lago Maggiore, a lake in northern Italy. My grandmother was a housewife, the best cook in the world, and equal parts gambler and sorceress. She could interpret dreams and talk to spirits. She was an incredibly inspiring person who lodged the idea in my mind that each woman is special and unique.

I graduated from college with a degree in film history and wrote my thesis on comic female archetypes. I focused on Mae West's career as a woman who did not feel obliged to subordinate herself to "rules" of gender roles. Mae West was irreverent and daring. She was provocative and cutting edge. She wrote her own dialogues to be more effective in delivering her lines, which had an irresistible comic effect.

I started working as an apprentice journalist for the staff of a women's magazine before I even graduated from college. I was particularly interested in researching real people with interesting lives, and I spent my time reading everything I could get my hands on: newsletters, foreign magazines, books. I was always coming across interesting characters, and I took the privilege my job afforded me to contact these unusual people and request interviews. I became particularly fond of interviewing and profiling, but the magazines I worked for through the years were not always willing to send me out across oceans and borders to chase these people down.

And so it was after only a few years that I decided to leave behind my nine-to-five job and live my life as the adventure I wanted it to be. I became a freelance writer and reporter. I was my own boss and I was truly free. Freedom, I realized, was worth much more to me than money and security. I felt happy and relaxed. I didn't fear anything, as long as I could follow my dreams. I felt my calling was to be a storyteller. I decided that I would travel the world, seeking out those who had life stories that needed to be told. Some of those stories were men's. But I was drawn to the women I met time and time again.

Reckless

I've met a lot of interesting women through the past twenty years. I flew from Italy to Peru to meet Maria Reiche, the custodian of the mysterious Nazca lines inscribed on the Nazca Desert. I flew to Bejing, China, to meet the first woman mayor of Canton. I visited the leader of the S&M prostitutes in Hamburg, Germany, and I flew to Wisconsin to meet Jeana Yaeger after her landing with the *Voyager*, the aircraft she built with her then-companion, Dick Rutan, to circumnavigate the world nonstop in 1986 (they did it in nine days, three minutes, and forty-four seconds, establishing a Guinness world record). I spent incredible days in Chicago with Leonora Carrington, the surrealist painter and companion of Max Ernst during World War II.

I paid out of pocket for every one of these trips without hesitation. And in the end I never regretted having done it. Meeting these incredible people was worth every penny and every minute of my time. They motivated me even more than I was already driven to pursue my own dreams. They gave me strength and courage. They made me feel privileged and reinforced my idea that fear is the worst trap of all. I wanted to be as fearless as I had been as a little girl with dreams of a future that knew no bounds—and I was. At twenty, thirty, and now forty, I can still say that I am living a fearless life. I have lived my life not by the limits dictated by fear, but by the infinite possibilities born of excitement.

My globetrotting in search of inspiring people also gave me the opportunity to write this book. Of all the women I met, I selected nine to be included in this collection of life stories. These are women who took up challenges to better themselves. They pushed their limits and overcame their fears. They live as great adventurers ruled by desire, not by stereotypes. They escape definition and refuse to be labeled. They are strong as nails, yet flexible in their approach to their chosen challenges.

Introduction

Libby Riddles was the first woman to win the legendary Iditarod, the dog-sled race from Anchorage to Nome, after a century of male victories. Twin sisters Angelika Castaneda and Barbara Warren are Ironman, X Games, and triathlon multichampions. They are now just over sixty years old. Gevin Fax left a promising career in Ohio, jumped on her Harley-Davidson, and cruised to California, where she became the ambassador of women bikers. Julia Butterfly Hill lived alone for more than a year in Humboldt County, California, atop an ancient giant sequoia tree that loggers had slated to cut down. She risked her own life to save Luna, the tree she had come to cherish. Lisa Distefano was the captain of a pirate vessel that rammed fishing boats on the hunt for whales and seals. Polly Matzinger has become a world-renowned biologist at forty-six, after previous careers as a cocktail waitress and a dog trainer. Wilma Mankiller was chief of the Cherokee Nation of Oklahoma for more than ten years. Annie Duke is the queen of professional poker tournaments and plans to send her four children to Columbia University with the earnings from her gambling career.

I traveled from Alaska to Oklahoma, from Maryland to Northern California, and from Las Vegas to Washington State to seek out these inspiring women. I spent time with them, often for days or weeks at a time, thanks to what I consider to be my good fortune. I shared their enthusiasm for living life to the fullest. I continue to travel the world collecting unusual stories because my own adventure is my call to storytelling. When I was five, I didn't play with Barbie like the other girls. Instead, I would climb trees and settle in the lustrous foliage, telling myself the story of my soon-to-be-adventurous life. I would spend whole afternoons picturing myself strolling through Mars's reddish, sandy, bubbling mounds, fully equipped with a (sexy!) astronaut suit. Sometimes I would imagine myself sailing along coasts where indigenous people with features like none I had ever seen would come greet me and welcome me to their homeland. Other times I was on top of the mountains, wrapped in fluffy white clouds or on some distant but equally deserted, crackling, icy shores. Sometimes I was a trapeze artist. Other times I was a pirate. Whatever or wherever I was, my crew was always an all-woman team.

When I was eleven, I heard the lyrics of "Born to Be Wild" for the first time. In that moment I had an epiphany. "Get your motor runnin' / Head out on the highway / Lookin' for adventure / And whatever comes our way." I wanted my life to be like the lyrics of that song. When I turned twenty, all it took was one sentence for me to fall in love with Karen Blixen. I instantly became her follower because of a single passage in which she described the essence of youth as the conviction of being invincible. Her idea that feeling invincible was the true fountain of youth transfixed my soul and imagination. It was the spear of a sober and secular revelation, striking my mind with the electric power of lightning.

Dreaming is a call to adventure, inviting us to escape the barriers that daily life can impose on us. Dreaming is perhaps the only right that can't be taken away from prisoners. Dreaming is the ability not only to point your finger at the moon, but to hitchhike all the way up there. Could the full moon ever be canned? No way. Dreaming puts the spark in your eye when you're ready to lift your spirit away from the misery of a non-dreamer's life.

I've always been interested in dreamers, those who are able to deconstruct all the caging rules and switch their mental functions at the drop of a hat. Paying no respect to traditional roles is emphasized all the more by women who choose to bend the rules. They playfully switch the paths of queens and kings on the checkerboard. Women dreamers could not care less about showing that they're emancipated or "equal," because their world is not a satellite spinning around a male source of light. They thrive on being winners. They face the enemy straight on, even when the enemy is fear. They fall. They fail. They get up and go on again. They succeed. They live every day as if it is their last. Is it because they've been diagnosed with a terminal illness? Yup: They are *terminally alive*, as every being should be, every day. They're heroes. They laugh away misery by attempting to ambush their own existence. They're crazy wise women, according to the definition provided my friend Tom Robbins, who once gave me the following insight about this particular branch of wisdom:

> *Crazy wisdom is a bit difficult to explain but, fundamentally, it is that wisdom that is the opposite of conventional wisdom. Wisdom that deliberately swims against the current, goes against the flow.*
>
> *Wisdom that refuses to toe any party line. Wisdom that insists on choosing the short end of the stick, and breaks taboos in order to destroy their power. It is the wisdom of taking risks and living free, a wisdom of inspired playfulness, a contrary wisdom, a wisdom that turns the table on bourgeois seriousness and its ultimate repression of the human spirit. It is reflected in the behavior not of the suicidal hero giving up his life in order to change the world, but of the survivor clown, who manages to enjoy life under the most difficult of conditions and changes society by mocking and making fun of its stupidities and evils. We practice crazy wisdom whenever we break out of the mold and do the unexpected, and by so doing become more truly alive. . . .*
>
> *In enlightened play, the player turns his or her attention away from the rules and conventions of ordinary daily existence and dares to embrace the*

Reckless

extraordinary. If they have turned seriously enough—
have turned with intelligence as well as with wild
humor—they will have recreated reality and will have
developed the capacity to see the face of the Divine in
all things. And they will have a hell of a good time.

The women profiled in this book are women warriors, and they are reckless. At the same time, they can be the most self-disciplined creatures you'll ever meet. They are dynamic. And dynamite! They believe in evolution. They don't believe in being controlling or being controlled by others. This recalls another bit of wisdom that Tom Robbins once shared with me:

> *Evolution doesn't have an outline, an ultimate plan.*
> *Evolution is making it up as it goes along. However,*
> *there's a great intelligence operating behind that free-*
> *wheeling creativity. Another example would be the*
> *playfulness of the Zen master, the Taoist saint,*
> *the Sufi master, the Tantric guru. Theirs is the kind*
> *of play that lifts one out of social, political and eco-*
> *nomic context and puts one in contact with a higher*
> *dimension of reality that interfaces with the Mystery.*
> *Such actions may appear silly on the surface, espe-*
> *cially to those hundreds of millions of earthlings who*
> *are dull-witted and hidebound, yet they serve to help*
> *keep the world lively and give it*
> *the flexibility to endure.*

I am drawn to women who follow their own direction, are coherent, and get things done without fearing contradictions. When Julia Butterfly Hill told me that she was dreaming of celebrating her next birthday submerged in hot, bubbling, perfumed bathtub water and surrounded by scented candles, cushy pillows, and fluffy throws, I was that much more taken with her. She told me so while mending holes in the double-thick socks that she wore inside her military sleeping bag to keep her calloused feet from freezing at night.

I liked Lisa Distefano even more when she confessed to me that she felt like a Cinderella with her Prince Charming the day she married Paul Watson, founder of Sea Shepherd and captain of the *Sirenian,* the twin vessel of Lisa's own ship. They watched each other through binoculars, not meeting for days at a time even though they were sharing the same strip of ocean. And yet Lisa felt like a fairy-tale princess.

Freya Stark, a magnificent explorer of old who did not stop wandering through mountains and deserts until her nineties, once wrote:

> *I grew up among painters and musicians but I did not*
> *show any talent for both arts. Yet, there was in me an*
> *impulse strong as love and deep as life, which was*
> *asking to be expressed some way. I forged my future*
> *as the sculptor forges clay and I decided not to fear*
> *anything. I was insensitive to danger, since*
> *my goal was to end my days free from the*
> *weakness of a bourgeois life.*

The only norm is no norm at all. If you want to follow in these reckless women's footsteps, the only talent you need is a talent for living. Every one of these women shows no fear of isolation and yet does not use it to barricade herself from the rest of the world. Relationships are so much nicer when they're not born out of symbiotic need but spring from desire and are kept alive by choice. That's the wisdom of wild, uncaged crea-tures. As animals in the wilderness, these women don't just "respect" nature, they love it deep in their bones. They nour-ish their souls by watching the open landscape. They breathe in the scent of moist shrubbery early in the morning. They smell rain in the air before it starts pouring. They can use a starry sky as a compass and still be crazy about technology. They're good with tools. Computer screens, cellular phones, digital cameras, electric treadmills—these are the perfect complements to crashing waves, howling winds, open roads, and snowcapped peaks. The future and the present are flowing, and life is simmering in the existential kettle of global evolution. There have been reckless women since the beginning of time. Today, however, being born to be wild does not necessarily imply that one must remain an outsider, watching from shore while the bubbling current of evolution passes by. Progress is not the enemy of creativity. Success is not antithetical to individual free expression.

Reckless women are pioneers by nature. Anything completely new is attractive; ever exciting, never worrisome. The body is a temple for imagination and desire. Life is a wild game. And it's a woman's game too.

—Gloria Mattioni
  June 2005
  Los Angeles, California

Sled Dog Champion

LIBBY RIDDLES

I am frozen to the bone, despite the multiple layers of thermal undergarments and heavy sweaters I wear underneath my big down jacket. The silhouette of the small plane that dropped me here on a white, treeless prairie is now a distant speck against the cloudy sky. The only indications of any altitude as far as my eyes can see are mounds of wet snow. *This world is wet and flat,* I think as I search to find a single three-dimensional object that might stand out against the monochromatic background. Silence is thick, to the point that I can actually hear the buzz of the light rain.

I am still struggling to regain control of my stomach, which was deeply upset by the ups and downs of the rocky, seventy-five-minute, tighter-than-usual airbus flight to this remote part of the world. I futilely attempt to walk fast, but it's a Humpty Dumpty walk caused by the excessive weight of my clothes. I keep my eyes on the road. There are unexpected pitfalls, such as openings in the icy crust that make a rubbery noise under my boots and threaten to delay my already-slow progress.

My ride should be here soon, I hope. I had called ahead of time from Italy and made contact with Pete, the owner of Nome Country Store, who promised to send someone to get me from the small airport landing. The driver can only come from one direction, thankfully, so I plow steadily down the open rode, rather than freeze while I wait. I sent word to Pete last night from Anchorage, having just arrived from a relatively decent flight in comparison to what I experienced on my way to Nome.

Nome, once an Eskimo village on the south coast of the Seward Peninsula facing Norton Sound, the bay that opens on to the Bering Sea, is proud to be Alaska's oldest first-class city, incorporated on April 9, 1901. Alaska became a full-fledged state in January 1959 after having been discovered in 1741 by Vitus Bering and later purchased from Russia by the United States for $7,200, which amounted to 2.5 cents per acre for a state twice the size of Texas. Today, with a population of approximately three thousand, Nome is not really much of a city. It remains a very remote, tiny place, appealing mostly to natives or the occasional outsider like Libby Riddles, the woman who, in 1985, won the toughest and longest sled-dog race in the world—the Iditarod.

The news of her victory is what inspired me to come way out to this desolate part of the world, where she lives alone with her dogs. Nome was one of the few places where Libby felt she could achieve the silence, solace, and concentration necessary for her difficult training. I read about Libby's stunning heroism in the American press; I was living in Italy at the

2

time, and I had taken to reading American news for my work with the various magazines that employed me. I was always searching for interesting people and adventures, and when I read about Libby, I was in awe of her. I wanted to meet her immediately, but it took me two years—until 1987—to arrange to get to Alaska.

Most of Libby's Iditarod competitors were tough men renowned for their physical strength and daring spirit. *Imagine their surprise*, I thought, *when a slender, resilient young woman became the first female ever to win the race after more than half a century of male victories.* The race began in celebration of the sled dogs who, in 1925, rushed nonstop through storms and in freezing temperatures to cover the more than one thousand miles between Anchorage and Nome. They had good reason to rush: They were taking emergency medical supplies to Nome during a time when many of its residents' lives were threatened by a diphtheria epidemic. The Iditarod later became a very important sporting event on the endurance race circuit, boasting its own peculiar mythology.

It was amazing to see Libby there among the male competitors—the winner! I remember seeing the picture of her and her two pack-leader dogs, their heads peeking out from a lei of red roses delivered to the winning team after they came trotting past the finish line. The biting cold turned Libby's nose as red as the roses. Her long blond hair blanketed one of her dogs' snouts as she leaned forward to kiss him. After all, Libby knew that she hadn't won the race alone. Her dedication to and treatment of her sled dogs was unparalleled; the veterinarians monitoring the race awarded her a Humanitarian Prize for being the most conscientious musher on the course.

As I stared at the picture, I could feel the bond between the woman and her dogs. *That must have been her secret,* I remember thinking at that time. She looked like a fairytale princess, which made it hard for me to picture her fighting the elements and toughing it out against burly men. Later I would learn that she went through many feelings—pain, sickness, and sometimes fear—all alone on that long and dangerous trail. Yet she won and gained the right to call herself a sled-dog race champion. She showed that yes, it takes guts, it takes focus, it takes courage—and a lot of self-discipline—but that it's indeed possible to be successful and live the life that you've always dreamed of.

Nome saw better days at the beginning of the twentieth century. The news of gold discovered at Anvil Creek in the mid-1900s reached the outside world and provoked an exodus of thousands from the ports of San Francisco and Seattle as soon as steamships could break the ice to reach the northern town. Tents covered the entire landscape between Cape Rodney and Cape Nome, which owes its name to a spelling mistake dating back to 1850. As the story goes, the officer of a British ship stationed off the Alaskan coast wrote "? Name" next to an unidentified but prominent point on a manuscript map. The draftsman assigned to copy the official map interpreted the "?" as a *c* and the *a* in "Name" as an *o,* thus christening the unidentified area as "Cape Nome," a misnomer that made it all the way to the final mapmaker for the British Admiralty.

In its heyday, the gold camp known as Nome offered shelter to almost twenty thousand gold-hunters. In 1900, the population reached its highest point, recorded as 12,488, and the U.S. census listed one-third of all whites living in Alaska as residents of Nome. Today—although all of its citizens make their living from means other than gold pan and

4

rocker, and very little gold-rush architecture has survived a multitude of fires and storms—only 58 percent of the population is native. Air travel has replaced the steamship as the chief mode of transport to Nome, and many adventurers who consider Alaska the ultimate American frontier arrive here fed up with big cities, traffic, and pollution in the hope of finding a different way of life. The immediate area is still rich in gold and minerals, and the Alaska Gold Company is still a major operating gold-mining agency. Oil and gas exploration in the Norton Sound are also flourishing, and Nome is the transportation and commerce center for northwest Alaska.

Tourism has also become an important part of the economic base, but travelers seldom visit only for the beautiful ivory the Eskimos carve. They go to Nome from all over America and other parts of the world to witness the 1,049-mile annual Iditarod that takes place in March. The Iditarod Trail spans from Anchorage to Nome and is one of the last major solo adventures of our times. All around Alaska, all year long, tales of the Iditarod are murmured in saloons and bars as hunters, fishermen, and oil workers gather after long, hard days of work to discuss the highlights and disasters of years past and ponder the newcomers to the annual race. They refer to the Iditarod dog winners with awe and admiration, as if they were all Buck, the indomitable and loyal dog celebrated by Jack London in *The Call of the Wild.* Buck's renowned feat was pulling a thousand-pound sled when his owner bet he could do it, much to the dismay of the clientele at the Eldorado Saloon in Dawson City.

They talk about the mushers, too, the men and women who race with their sled dogs and who got their name from the French command *marche.* And since 1985, the locals especially like to talk about Libby Riddles. Other women have

5

since won the Iditarod, some multiple times, but only one woman can ever claim to have broken the male streak and enabled others to follow in her footsteps.

I left Italy at the beginning of October without any assurance that I'd find Libby. I was wearing a t-shirt, sneakers, and blue jeans. Twenty-four hours later, here I am, jet lagged and walking in the middle of a white planet, so wrapped in layers that I look like a clumsy, stoned Michelin man, trusting the word of a store owner whom I have never even met. I hit the ice hard with my boots, trying to warm up my frozen feet. The cold, white wetness takes on the barest of dimensions as darkness sets in with the rapid setting of the midday sun, which only lasts for a few hours during this time of year.

The stillness and silence are finally broken by the idling noise of an engine. An old Dodge 4x4 truck appears on the road, suddenly close, seemingly out of nowhere in the blinding whiteness. Its long bed is full of freshly cut logs that roll back and forth; it rumbles as it gets closer. Here's my guy, sent my way by the Country Store owner, ready to rescue me. He delivers me to the doorstep of the one-room bed-and-breakfast run by Judith DeMarsh on L Street where Pete, the store owner, advised me to stay. He has assured me that Eskimos, who stop by there for their morning coffee, travel the route toward Libby's cabin and will agree to give me a lift. But even if I'm lucky enough to hitch a ride and cover the twenty-plus miles of trail—not even a dirt road—that leads to Libby's cabin, what do I do if she's not there? What will she think of a foreign journalist arriving unannounced on her doorstep?

6

What if is something I have to remove from my mind, since anxiety is not going to help a bit. Now all I can worry about is how to get out of my layers. The heater in the truck is working full blast, as is the radio, set on KICY FM 100, and they are aiding and abetting each other in giving me a mean headache. My rescuer, a redhead with a reddish-brown beard flowing to his chest, is wearing only a snug t-shirt under a flannel shirt with rolled-up sleeves. He makes a living chopping wood and cuts the perfect image of a logger with his giant, twenty-inch biceps, which he hasn't gotten just by pumping iron at a gym or injecting steroids. He keeps asking me questions, letting me understand that my rescue happened only by chance: He had stopped by the store to sell some wood, and the owner had asked him to pick me up. Nothing planned. Chance, I will learn, is the rule of thumb in this world. I have to pray for chance if I want to find Libby tomorrow. But chances are, I won't.

Judith DeMarsh's coffee deserves its reputation. Three cups of her black medicine wipe away that pounding headache that kept me tossing and turning all night. Judith rushes me out the door as soon as she spots a fast-flying shadow approaching from the east. The sled, which I hope bears my escort, stops in an elegant wide arc, spraying a mix of slush and mud. October mysteries: The weather is starting to warm up for a sudden memory of summer in midfall. Soon this place will become a mud trap, if fresh snow doesn't replace the currently dissolving layer.

We can still dogsled across the tundra to Libby's cabin— me, my Eskimo Santa, whose name is Kikkapoo, or maybe Kikkamoo, and his team of dogs. I hold on tight, my arms wrapped around Kikkapoo's waist, resting my right cheek against his upper back while we take off as if in flight. His body shields mine from the wind and the eternal drizzle, and though it limits my view, I am grateful. I can hear the dogs panting, but I cannot make out any sound of their paws hitting the ground. I hear only the *gee* and *haw* commands, for right and left, respectively, and the *swish* of the sled when we slalom through bumps and ditches. All my belongings are tightly packed in a small backpack that I brought as my airplane carry-on, yet it's heavy enough that I'm starting to feel its weight.

We stop when my teeth have just started rattling out of control and my hands are solidifying into two distinct cubes of ice, despite my supposedly guaranteed techno-clothing thermal gloves. Even if whining could do me any good, I still wouldn't dare. The primitive cabin I behold, encircled by about fifty doghouses made out of plywood boxes, is enough to make me swallow my pain and is worth my temporary transformation into a human ice statue. Not one telephone pole is in sight, not even a trace of power lines anywhere. Libby goes into town once a week to check her messages on an answering machine that the storekeeper allows her to keep there. It is her only communication channel with the rest of the world, since a "wired" Alaska is still more than ten years away. There are no other cabins in the visible vicinity. This is the most isolated house I've ever seen.

Outside the borders of this frozen universe, the world keeps spinning with its kaleidoscope of sounds and lights. Here everything is white and still. Here life assumes a totally different pace, and the priorities are not the same.

Later I learn that Libby had broken up with her Eskimo boyfriend and relocated to Nome from the nearby town of Teller, seventy miles north on the coast of the Bering Sea. She had left with a pack of dogs on a Cessna plane and bought a desolate piece of land with the remaining prize money from her 1985 victory, and she was determined to build a shelter for herself and her dogs. She chopped wood and cut logs to

8

build her own cabin. She single-handedly scared away bears attracted by the dog food, shooting her handgun high into the sky as a first warning. She bought building supplies from catalogs, since online shopping from Alaska wasn't an option in those days. She caught enough salmon to feed herself and her dogs through the winter, catching their supply before the river sealed itself under an icy crust.

Her homestead looks like a fort surrounded by the tents of a military outpost. The doghouses are chained to each other in a gang line, and every occupant is chained to his own doghouse. The dogs are all standing on their respective roofs, howling and barking to announce the arrival of strangers. These dogs are mutts, mostly Alaskan husky mixes, seemingly related to wolves. They don't look like the Siberian silver-furred variety. They are lean and muscular, between forty-five and fifty-five pounds each. Some of them have blue eyes, others have brown. A few of the most striking ones have one of each color. They wag their tails and bare their fangs simultaneously, while making a hell of a noise. I can easily picture huskies like these fighting a grizzly bear or a giant moose, as I have been told they do, if an emergency were to occur on the trail.

The noise must have given the alarm, and Libby Riddles appears on the porch steps as soon as I jump off the sled. Libby is an unlikely vision in this place; she'd fit better on the cover of a young women's magazine. Another *swish* and my carriage, driver, and reindeers are gone. Here I am, in front of a smiling woman and her growling dogs, trying to refresh her memory about my attempts to contact her. I could just as easily be thrown out or received for just an hour's visit. But Libby welcomes me very warmly. She's glad to see I've made it.

"You were for real, then," she says. "Since I won the Iditarod, I've been approached by many new people. Lots

9

of American journalists wrote me asking for interviews. But when they discovered that they couldn't reach me by a simple airline flight to Teller, they would just back out. Or I always had to go to Anchorage. Thanks to my victory, I'm sponsored by Alaska Airlines, so I can fly for free. But it isn't the same thing. To understand the reasons why I won, it's important to see this place. This," she waves at the surroundings, "is my world. This is my daily life, the life of a musher, a little-known profession outside these borders! Welcome to my world."

She opens the door to the house and bows her head to get through. I can step in without bending, since I'm a good three inches shorter than she is. Libby is tall, thin, and graceful. She's thirty-one, close to my own age. She's wearing corduroy pants and a bulky sweater. Once inside and warmed up after a steaming hot cup of tea and breakfast, she takes her sweater off to reveal her sinewy muscles. "I got buff lifting Pepsi-Cola cases onto a truck all winter long when I was sixteen. I had just arrived in Alaska, tired of student life in Minneapolis. I spent two seasons that way, working ten hours a day in Anchorage. Then, when spring came, I had enough money to fly out to this territory, the tundra. I was seeking freedom. I wanted to live close to nature and animals. I found all that, but I moved so many times and lived in so many houses. And I always lived with somebody else. When I turned thirty, I felt like I needed my own space. I wanted to build it my way. So here it is, my mansion!"

A clawfoot bathtub, which leans vertically against the wall of the living room, is the only hint of potential luxury inside the cabin. And since it still needs to be moved to the bathroom, there's not much to suggest that Libby needs a lot to keep her content. She's very proud of her recent acquisition; she thinks of it as the missing link, the finishing touch that will definitely transform the cabin into a heavenly retreat.

10

Hanging on the log panels of the living room are many pictures of family, friends, and countless dogs.

"This woman is Patty Friend. She gave me a lead on a summer job and some of her dogs, and, most important, inspiration. In 1979, running the Cantwell 180 sled-dog race, she sprinted to the finish half a minute ahead of the competition and became the first woman to win a long-distance sled-dog race. I thought of her when I was close to the end of the Iditarod, feverish and wet, and I still made the decision to run through the Shaktoolik checkpoint and throw myself back into a stormy hell. Lavon Barve, the musher who arrived there just after me, told me that I was crazy to continue and that I would never make it when I told him about my resolution. But I owed it to myself, to my dogs, and to the people of Teller who had trusted my judgment and ability to win. I could not lose my advantage. This time, I had to win."

Libby follows my eyes to a picture where she's standing behind her sled next to a companion musher. "This is Joe," she says with a smile. "Joe Garnie. He was my partner and boyfriend who I lived with in Teller. He was the mayor of that small community. Compared to Teller, Nome is a metropolis," she laughs. Libby and Joe bred and trained dogs to run the Iditarod. They shared the same team of dogs and traded dogs each year. In 1985, Libby had already raced in the Iditarod twice before. Since she and Joe were not rich and could not lead the more comfortable life of professional mushers like Susan Butcher, who had four times as many dogs and five men working for her, they had to earn their living in other ways.

Susan Butcher would win the Iditarod several times after Libby first broke the male streak. Libby and Susan have a professional relationship, each of them genuinely happy for the

11

other. Libby speaks of Susan with high regard and without any trace of jealousy. "We have different styles. But I have a lot of respect for her. I was sincerely sorry when, in 1985, she had to drop out during the second segment of the race, after only a hundred and fifty miles. A moose killed two of her dogs and injured several others. Susan had to withdraw, but all she cared about was the loss of those two good dogs."

Often, not enough money was left for Libby and Joe to pay the race entrance fee. In 1985, the Bingo Players Collective of Teller paid for Libby's $1,249 enrollment. Some of the other mushers already enrolled in the race tried to discourage the Bingo Players, pushing them to have Joe lead the team. But Joe Garnie stood up to the protests: "Don't underestimate her. She's going to pass you up." And his prediction proved true, despite the fact that Libby's supplies were more meager than the average musher's. Prior to the race, each musher has their equipment and food supplies airdropped to the eighteen checkpoints along the trail. Although Libby's loads were definitely the poorest and the worst, this minor setback didn't dampen her resourcefulness and courage. "One of those mushers, Rick Swenson, swore he'd walk from Nome all the way back to Anchorage the day a woman won the Iditarod. But he never did. Not when I won, and not later when Susan won."

Libby experienced several challenging and frightening incidents during the race, and she speaks with pride about her accomplishments and the obstacles she overcame. Shortly after Susan Butcher had to drop out because a moose killed two of her dogs, Libby encountered the same moose in the trail between Rabbit Lake and Finger Lake.

12

"It was dangerous," Libby recalls, "since he probably weighed fifteen hundred pounds. Kicking and stomping from a moose that size can cause the dogs to become entangled in

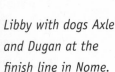

Libby with dogs Axle and Dugan at the finish line in Nome.

their own lines as they attempt to flee the dangerous situation. The moose stood there, staring us down. The dogs were trapped by their own harnesses, tied to the sled and to each other. I had decided to leave my .41 Ruger at home, so shooting him wasn't even an option had he decided to attack. But we got lucky. We were able to pass him by turning off the trail to the right, bypassing him and avoiding the confrontation. Cold shivers shot down my back, despite the fact that I was wearing my brand-new, super-insulated L.L. Bean jacket. The moose just stood his ground. He didn't make any attempts to come toward us."

Like all travelers in winter, moose prefer hard-packed trails to deep snow. And as large as they are, they are reluctant to yield ground. Many moose inhabit the lowlands between Knick and the Alaska Range, and moose spottings

13

Sled Dog Champion

are common among the racing teams that cover the trail. However, close encounters still incite fear in any musher. Libby recalls, "People asked me, 'Weren't you afraid?' Sure I was. But I didn't let fear stop me. People sometimes ask me if I'm afraid living out here all alone. Sometimes I think I enjoy the risks. I don't let possible danger stop me from enjoying the life I've always dreamed of."

Later on, after Libby and her team escaped their close encounter, another musher, Monique Bene, was knocked off her sled by a moose that stood over her for twenty minutes while she lay motionless in the snow. Eventually, the huge animal shuffled off, allowing her to move from her motionless position. She was lucky he left before she froze to death.

Moose are not the only danger on the trail. Of all things, it turned out that an old washing machine iced into the trail just a few miles outside of Anchorage was the first major pitfall for Libby and her team. "I had just crashed into another racer and his team, which ended up in the underbrush and had become entangled among the trees. I didn't stop in time, and my own dogs got snared in their own lines. We managed to get back on the trail after our misadventure, but because we had just freed ourselves from one mishap, I was taken by surprise by the next obstacle. Two by two, the dogs jumped over the washer to avoid hitting it face on. The sled hit hard, and I flew over the top." This was just one of several accidents that occurred on the very first day of the race. "I went flying into the sky more than once. I even lost my dog team at some point, when the whole group took off without me, uprooting the tree I had hitched them to when we had set up camp earlier.

"These dogs have power. They're not pets. They love to work. They love to run. In their eagerness to hit the trail, they can snap heavy ropes. With fourteen to eighteen dogs per team, the sled itself has the power of a bullet. One team

14

of ten dogs is known to have pulled at their harnesses with such vigor that they managed to drag a pickup truck some distance. And the truck was locked into first gear with the parking brake engaged!"

To explain better, Libby leads me in the shed where she keeps tools and sleds. Including the driver, a sled loaded for the Iditarod weights between three hundred and five hundred pounds. That means about thirty pounds per dog, which is actually less than the average driver's rule of thumb, which states that a dog should never pull more than its own weight. "When we train them," Libby tells me, "we teach them to trot at a pace of eleven to twelve miles per hour pulling that load. With an unloaded sled, they are free to set their own pace."

Libby lifts a tarp to reveal an eclectic collection of equipment. "Here's my cooker. All the salmon, lamb, beef, and chicken for the dogs must be sliced thin, frozen, and shipped in advance to the different checkpoints. You retrieve it and cook it there. Then you put the leftovers in a cooler to keep it warm for the next day or so, until the next checkpoint." Race rules require the driver to show that he or she carries at least two pounds of dog food per dog, and a day's food ration for the musher, before leaving each checkpoint. "You also need feeding pans, a dipper for loading dog food, tools for sled repairs, spare lines and harnesses, electrical tape, a shovel and an axe, chains to tie injured or exhausted dogs to the sled, headlamps and batteries, a compass, topographical maps, and personal toiletries. But what you most need"—she digs in a canvas bag and extracts what looks like a handmade baby shoe—"are doggie booties." She tells me that hundreds of them are necessary to protect those paws from ice balls that form between the pads separating their digits. The many miles of trail that run over sea ice, with its blanket of granular snow, can wreak havoc on the dogs' paws.

Sled Dog Champion

Libby continues, "A woman friend of mine helped me sew all of them. Hours and hours of preparation, just for this one little thing." Another female neighbor taught Libby how to cook "Eskimo ice cream," made with grease from reindeer meat, seal oil, salmon eggs, and sugar. "A lot of calories are packed into a few spoonfuls, and it keeps you going for a long while," Libby assures me.

Yet another Teller woman suggested sewing a miniature alarm into Libby's hat, so that she could wake up after just an hour's sleep and slip away, leaving the other mushers asleep at the checkpoint and giving herself a bit of an advantage. "Sometimes it's better to sleep outdoors on your own sled, wrapped in your arctic sleeping bag, than at the checkpoint with the other racers. The Iditarod is an endurance as well as a speed race, after all."

Endurance is certainly called for. Every year, more than sixty mushers leave the starting line, but only half of them arrive at the finish. The weather is severe and the terrain ever changing. From Anchorage, in the south-central part of the state, the trail winds through spruce and birch forest, crossing frozen lakes and bogs, following meandering rivers toward their sources in the Alaska Range. South of the range, the weather is relatively temperate. The trail rises into the mountains to Rainy Pass at almost 3,200 feet. Just to the North stands Mount McKinley, the tallest peak in North America at 20,320 feet. And even worse than the mountains is the Great Interior, Jack London's land of icy silence, where temperatures that reach the negative-30s are common and the potential to dip into the negative-50s and even -70s is not unknown.

The trail runs along portions of the Kuskokwim River. Forests and tundra alternate until the trail reaches the Yukon River, also known as the Mississippi of Alaska. Here the teams are greeted by northern winds of more than fifty miles per

16

hour that worsen the effect of the already-frigid temperatures. Then, after rising again to cross a low pass in the Nulato Hills, the trail drops to the Bering Sea coast and a third climate, somewhat tempered by the ocean. Teams may face the danger of going out on thin ice or being swept out to sea on an ice floe. As the racers near Nome, at the end of these very intense thousand miles, high winds howling out of valleys along the Seward Peninsula are powerful enough to overturn sleds and knock dogs off their feet.

Daylight is rapidly withdrawing from the sky beyond the shed, and a whining, howling chorus starts up. "Dinnertime!" Libby announces. She spots me glancing at my watch, and she clarifies, "Daylight is not guaranteed every day in Alaska. Once, in Teller, we didn't see any light for seventy-two hours straight. Not the best cure for anxiety. But you can see wonders like the aurora borealis and a midnight sun here. So I guess not everything about it is bad." She puts on yellow-rubber waterproof overalls and a hat outfitted with a flashlight. She asks me to help her fill up the buckets with water from the tank that she replenishes each time she goes to the river. Other buckets are lined up next to them that need to be filled with dog food.

When we drag the buckets out to the dogs' kingdom, we're greeted with unabashed enthusiasm. The dogs wag their tails and jump on the roofs of their houses, as high as their chains allow them. Food is served to each dog on the ground. They can eat only when Libby gives them the "go" command. Libby has advised me in advance not to pet the dogs during feeding time, and that I'll be able to spend more quality time with them later, when she brings a couple of them into the house to sleep.

"They take turns sleeping inside, and they know that

17

they will each have the privilege sooner or later. That's the special time when I talk to them and thank them for being so good to me.

"I came to Alaska for a man. . . ." Libby laughs as she remembers. We are back in the warm cabin; the dogs' dinner has been served. "But I didn't stay because of him or any other man. I stayed for the dogs. I still can't get over how loyal, proud, and brave these dogs are," she says stroking the head of Axle, one of her team leaders from the 1985 Iditarod. He is curled up at her feet with Inca, another dog who was part of the '85 team. Tonight, they are the chosen couple.

"Look!" Libby opens a big book full of dog pictures. "Here I have each one of them and their genealogy. I could never guess, otherwise, which is the son or brother of another. Not for all of them, anyway." She turns the pages and stops at a picture of four dogs. "Dugan, Axle, Bugs, and Binga," she beams. "These four brothers were the core of my team. Then we had Dusty and Sister to help out," she says, pointing to another photo. Pages turn to photographs of countless other dogs. "Dusty was Joe's leader, his pride and joy," she tells me, pointing at a stout little red dog, more golden lab than husky. "He was a giveaway from our neighbor, Albert Oquillik. He was crazy for Joe; he would do figure eights and backflips for him. He served me well, too, in training and racing, but he was never as happy with me as he was with Joe. I guess he was a one-person dog." More pages, more names: Ugly. Brownie. Socks. Stewpot. Each name designates a different personality and a unique story. "Socks was the smallest dog on the team, but built solid and strong. She could have been a bit faster, but somehow, with her short legs, she got the job done and she was consistent."

The dogs' personalities and builds are big factors in the lineup. They usually run in pairs, but occasionally a single

18

dog can run among the team, as was the case with Libby's team in 1985 when she raced with fifteen dogs. The leaders are the brains and the steering wheel. They set the pace and get their teammates moving at their speed by keeping the gang line taut. They also must show some ability to find and stay on the trail, feeling the packed snow underneath loose snow. The two dogs behind the leaders are called swing dogs, and they help steer by staying on the trail and forcing the rest of the team to turn in wide arcs that bring the sled around corners safely. Then there are several pairs of dogs who comprise the core team. They need to be strong and consistent and able to follow the pack. The last two dogs in line are wheel dogs. Their main function lies in their size. They are the largest animals on the team, since they bear the extra burden of being closest to the load of the sled, and they are the ones who pull the most weight when the sled moves uphill. They also need to be steady in temper, for the constant pounding of the other competitors close behind them can be unnerving.

"However, sometimes," adds Libby, "you need to move the dogs around. Two dogs can develop a dislike for each other and need to be separated, or a female coming into heat may have to be moved away from males." Racing huskies are not neutered or spayed, since their litters are highly desirable by mushers eager to find more good runners. "Also, a single lead dog could do better under certain conditions, or a single wheel dog may well offer more control of the sled on twisty trails."

Another page, another picture. It's Libby, sporting her "46" number across her back, ready to start the race with her packed sled and her excited team of dogs, still unaware that they are destined to be winners. It looks like she is a good forty feet from her lead dogs, and forty feet, I realize, is quite a distance to control during turns. "You need some skills," admits Libby with her typical modesty, "but most of all, you need

19

Sled Dog Champion

authority. You need to gain the respect of your dogs. They must trust you with their lives, since their lives and your own life depend on you. You must be like an oracle, able to predict the weather changes and dangers, but also like a fighter. On the trail, you are the general and your dogs are your soldiers. Your team is your army.

"Get up, you soldiers!" Even before she motions to the dogs to stand up, they have already made a dash for their bowls. Libby fills them with fresh water and explains, "They need so much water! In winter, I have to break the ice to get it out of the river. It's not easy. Nothing is easy here. Yet it is these daily challenges that you have to endure to survive that transform the routine of an ordinary life into an epic existence.

"And life becomes so much more enjoyable! It acquires a flavor that I certainly never tasted while living comfortably in Minnesota."

EPILOGUE

Long after my visit, when I enjoyed Libby's warm hospitality for a full weekend at her cabin, Libby kept training and racing. She now lives in a much bigger house near Homer, another Alaskan town, where she runs Blazing Kennels and raises future sled dog champions. Libby still trains and sometimes races. When she's not getting ready herself, she helps other mushers with their dogs' necessities.

She has authored three books and given lectures to colleges and conventions. In 2005, she hosted the local cable television show during the Iditarod. She has her own website and receives lots of letters from all over the world, from kids who want to know more about her adventures with her dogs.

LIBBY RIDDLES

She's never thought of stopping, leaving Alaska, or quitting her dog world. "It's my life now. All I can do is tell others the story of how beautiful it is living in it."

Sled Dog Champion

Twin Triathletes

ANGELIKA CASTANEDA & BARBARA WARREN

Summer 1996. A friend from Italy comes to visit me in Los Angeles. He brings a treasure, a tape recording of the final day of the X Games, a weeklong sports festival sponsored by ESPN. I've heard about the daredevils who compete in this 350-mile extreme adventure through four states in five days, but I haven't watched the live broadcast. I am in for a big surprise.

The tape starts rolling, and the screen goes from blue to chalk white and fades into a close-up of the pale face of a middle-aged blond woman. She's fighting to hold her grip on the hooks embedded in a steep wall of rocks. She's hanging off a cliff, not far from the top. Sweat is streaming from her forehead. The square muscle in her jaw is twisting in spasm. The commentator announces

23

that fifty-three-year-old Angelika Castaneda has sprained her left knee ligament only a few minutes before. The pain must be excruciating. She is a professional adventure racer who has competed on teams with Navy Seals. She's known for her abilities and strength, but this might be too much— even for her.

Sweat mixing with tears of frustration, Angelika cries out. It is heartbreaking to hear, like listening to the desperate cry of a wounded animal that has to admit to her weakness and defeat. But the sound ceases as quickly as it escaped. Then, in a shocking display of will, Angelika raises her head again. Her eyes lock with the top of the mountain, considering the distance she has to go if she wants to avoid elimination. She clenches her fists and starts to drag her body up. She's pushing with only one leg, using her strong arms to lift herself up. She's slow yet determined. She will not stop or give up. She climbs more, biting her lip as she pushes harder, her shoulder muscles contracting and tensing like guitar strings. She makes it to the top.

It's a triumph of will power. The spectators' applause is thunderous when her two teammates, New Zealanders John Francis Howard, age forty, and Keith Murray, age thirty-four, carry Angelika in their arms to their canoe. They still have to cross a swamp, a final paddle through the last stretch of the race. Angelika, exhausted, can only hunch forward and place her head in her hands.

Yet despite all obstacles, you can read victory on their faces even before they pass the finish line.

"She's a really gutsy woman," Keith Murray tells the television reporter at the finish line, after Angelika's team has won the race. *She is incredible,* I think; double incredible, as I would soon find out. I decided to seek her out as soon as the tape ended. I was drawn to Angelika. Something inside told me I had to look for her, talk to her.

ANGELIKA CASTANEDA & BARBARA WARREN

Angelika was something to behold. She reminded me of a cartoon character—the sporty, strong, sexy, powerful superheroine of my childhood fantasies—I used to draw and make paper cutouts of when I was a little girl in Italy. Her tall, slender body was richly endowed with lean muscle. Her super-short hair was dyed in two contrasting colors: bleach-blond on top, chestnut brown on the nape of her neck and the sides. Top that off with piercing blue eyes and a big, inviting smile. The first day we met, she was dressed in a skintight, electric-blue and fire-red bodysuit with blue tights. She was a modern-day version of Wonder Woman. Here was Angelika, my heroine in flesh and bones, muscle and spirit, anything but a paper doll. She was quick to smile anytime she talked about one of the many things she's fond of.

"I do everything with my sister," she informed me. As it turned out, Angelika, in all her extraordinariness, is not unique. She comes with a perfectly sculpted, equally athletic identical twin. Same look. Same age. Same dreams. Same drive and strong will.

They both lived in San Diego, a mere hundred miles from my house. Angelika and her sister and partner, Barbara Warren, agreed to see me together. As soon as I entered the house and the conversation started, it was clear that they think in unison. They talked at me together, with the same vitality and enthusiasm. They swept me off my feet with a tornado of energy spinning out of their mouths.

In 1996, the endurance circuit was still considered an outsiders' tournament compared to more popular competitions. The twins, therefore, though well known among extreme sports fans, had not yet achieved superstar status. Very few knew about the twins' achievements or even their existence, for that matter.

Twin Triathletes

I would soon find out that they had started their athletic career after turning forty, information that increased my already high regard and admiration for the twins. What better demonstration that you can be invincible, no matter how old you are? The Big Four-O is when most people feel it's time to start slowing down, with middle age just around the corner. Not the twins.

Over the next several years, I would make the hundred-mile drive between San Diego and L.A. many times. The twins had newly devoted their energy to an all-woman expedition to circumnavigate the world, using any sporting means, in two thousand hours to celebrate the year 2000. Their enthusiasm was contagious, and I found myself devoting much of my own time to the idea. Though the Women World Expedition was never realized, we spent long and pleasant hours dreaming and scheming in preparation, getting to know each other, sharing our worlds. It was exciting to get lost in hours and hours of conversations at Angelika's house perched atop a canyon, children and friends going to and from the pool and improvising jam sessions. I could see the admiration for these very special moms in the eyes of their teens. I could feel the warmth that these two women emitted to all the children, making them feel accepted and at ease.

We often discussed the twins' philosophy that age is just a state of mind. For Angelika and Barbara, the second phase of one's life is an opportunity to push the most toward new goals. They saw middle age as a coming into their own, a time to set new challenges in order to experience the adrenaline rush of feeling alive and vibrant, engaging every cell of the body and mind. They knew that the way to keep young was to engage the body and mind, and that being young at heart and in the mind is deeper than the lines that start cracking

ANGELIKA CASTANEDA & BARBARA WARREN

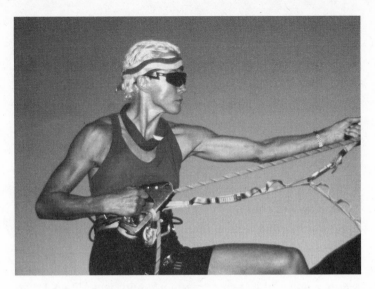

 Angelika climbing

once-youthful-looking faces or the pull of gravity that turns once-perky breasts southward. With so many exciting things to remember and so many others to look forward to, the mind keeps active and memories don't fade away.

"Who could enjoy a repetitive daily existence, predictable in each step?" Barbara asks the students attending her workshop entitled "How to Be a Winner in Life." In addition to being a multichampion, Barbara has a doctorate in psychology. Angelika, who never earned her bachelor's degree, has never felt outshined by her sister. The twins each support the other's decisions, complementing each other in their similarities and differences.

Barbara and Angelika thrive on the feverish emotion they achieve from challenging themselves to accomplish ambitious goals. Growing up in an isolated Austrian village called Saint Johann, forgotten by the outside world, the twins felt constricted by their small universe, guarded by the mountains to the point of near invisibility. They spent hours at the window of their childhood home, their gaze fixed on the far-off unknown beyond those peaks. That was the edge of their world, which the two of them identified as the "horizon," a horizon of freedom and excitement that beckoned from far beyond those loathed borders, just waiting for the two of them to come running.

Birth was the twins' first act of separation. Barbara arrived six hours after Angelika's first war cry in this world. During their upbringing in that remote alpine village and later during their adventurous lives, the twins have been separated by measures of hours, minutes, or seconds many times. In competitions, ranging from the Ironman, triathlons, and pentathlons to the X Games and other endurance races, Angelika and Barbara often follow on each other's heels. If one wins first place, the other soon follows.

In 1996, Angelika competed in ESPN's X Games without her sister. Barbara was there to support and encourage her, as the most affectionate of all coaches. From my seat on the couch that first day I ever saw Angelika compete, her endeavor looked heroic and authentic enough to raise the hair on my neck. But Barbara later told me that she could actually feel what her sister was feeling. Watching her sister cry out in pain but still looking up, her goal in sight, Barbara experienced pride and anguish. Angelika gritted her teeth and forced her body to push more and keep climbing, envisioning her team passing the finish line. And so they did, soon after. They won, thanks to a woman who doesn't understand the concept of giving up.

When they were little girls, the twins longed to explore that mysterious, unknown world that, in their minds, was just waiting for them. But why was that world beckoning just the two of them? They had another sister and two older brothers who didn't feel the same calling. They loved their family. They worshipped their mother, Ingrid, who brought up all five children on her own. Yet they had this fierce independence inscribed on their chromosomes, and they could not betray their nature. They knew they would have to look for adventure where adventure was. And they would have to go together, feeding on each other's wills. They were tied to each other still, as if breathing through the same umbilical cord.

It would always be that way.

Their strength grows from each other's energy. Power increases when one sister mirrors the other in words, thought, or action. Face to face they are identical, and their spirit is cut from the same cloth—a superwoman who grew two heads and two sets of arms and legs.

They couldn't wait to leave Austria, but abandoning their mother was painful. "She was our role model, our inspiration," say the sisters. "She raised us in hiding after our father was captured during World War II. He was taken away to a prison camp." Their mother not only climbed with her children to safety but also reestablished the family in their small village and continued hiking and climbing throughout their childhood, providing for her children by trekking out into the mountains beyond the village. She, too, is an adventurous spirit, and she never lost the taste for a challenge.

"She was still skiing and swimming in the icy waters of mountain lakes on her eightieth birthday. She swam outdoors even in winter, saying it kept her body toned. She likes to keep her mind toned, too. For her eightieth birthday, she bought herself a computer and learned how to communicate with us by email, marveling at the instant postcards that would cross the oceans in a second, eating up the distance. She's still cheerful and enthusiastic, like a kid."

So are the twins. They're quick to get excited, and they

smile and laugh a lot, but they can get serious and focused in a snap, and they're strong like rocks in difficult situations. They are still, in many ways, the same two brave fourteen-year-old girls who, many decades earlier, left home and the mountains they felt so ambivalent about.

Their journey took them first to Florence, Italy, to study fine arts. To pay for tuition, they modeled for fashion magazines like *Vogue* and *Harper's Bazaar.* Later they followed their new obsession with pre-Colombian art to Mexico, where they stood out with their long, slim legs, Nordic blue eyes, and blond pigtails that fell to their waists—their very *twinness.* Fashion following rules of its own, Barbara-Heidi and Angelika-Heidi soon became the most sought-after models in the business.

Barbara surpassed her sister in her paradox. She changed her last name from Muller to Angely. She sported black liquid eyeliner and a black wig, a black catsuit and a gun, and she became the bad-girl movie star of more than thirty Mexican films. Angelika, always the eclectic one, stayed in the fashion world but turned to design while also painting and choreographing ballet. She was featured in eighteen underwater documentaries as a scuba diver and free diver, and she doubled as Farrah Fawcett in the movie *Sundown.* Meanwhile, together in the same adventure once again, the two sisters opened a charm school, appealing to young girls wanting to follow in their footsteps and be models or actresses.

Fame was kind to the twins in the beginning, and they were gratified. "It felt good," says Angelika, "looking back and remembering those long afternoons looking through the windows, past the mountains in front of our house, imagining all the city lights that must be there, somewhere beyond the borders of our small world. Now, suddenly, all the spotlights were on us in Mexico City. Now we were getting invited to parties, were courted by the socialites. It was sweet for a little while . . . until boredom set in."

ANGELIKA CASTANEDA & BARBARA WARREN

They were both married with children by then, Angelika with two boys, Barbara with two girls. They longed for the comfort of a normal life. Hungry for privacy and tired of the Mexican jet set, they set off for their own version of adventure again. This time, in the early 1980s, they moved to the United States, where their respective husbands had already initiated some flourishing business relationships.

For the first time in their lives, Angelika and Barbara were separated for more than hours. It was inevitable: Barbara's husband was heading to Texas with his five kids from another marriage, plus the two daughters he had with Barbara, in tow, while Angelika's husband's business had landed them in San Diego. The twins started their new lives in two different American cities, facing all these changes without each other's reassuring presence. It was hard. It was new. It was frightening, for the first time.

"Barbara would write me letters," Angelika remembers, "telling me that she was interested in participating in a marathon. That was her new goal, and she started training to achieve it on her own. So I started running, too, as it seemed the right thing to do. If she was running, I should run. But my mind was somewhere else. My marriage was going downhill at high speed, and I felt very lonely. My confidence was blinking on and off like never before. I started running, I think, to recover that feeling of invincibility that had invigorated me in my younger years. I went looking for it in those beautiful canyons, breathing in the fresh scent of eucalyptus and pine trees, wishing to feel what I had felt while running in the mountains of my childhood."

Soon after, Barbara went through a divorce of her own and moved to San Diego. Angelika recalls, "I had just gotten a divorce myself. Life was handing us separation and reunion

31

at the same time. I felt like jumping out of my skin. My sister was going to be close to me again. We could go for those wild dreams again. Barbara's dream was to compete in running races. Did I want to share her dream? I did indeed. But she had already been training for five years. If I wanted to be her match, I'd have to push myself really hard. I would have to give my body and soul to that new goal. I would have to work harder than Barbara to get to the same place. *Well,* I thought, *wasn't that already our story since birth?* I was the one who had paved the way for her to be born. She had only had to slip out, following my lead! This time, she was leading. But I was going to push hard to catch up."

It's fascinating to watch Barbara and Angelika tease each other, savoring the taste of competition without jealousy. In the past twenty years, they've both won gold and silver medals and awards, together and separately. The inseparable duo baptized themselves the "Twin Team," and competed together in world championships, including the Triple Ironman, the Hawaiian Triathlon and Ironman, the Double Ironman, the Raid Gauloises in the Sahara Desert, and other endurance expeditions—tough competitions in extreme conditions in which exposure to the elements and fatigue claim many victims. Some people have to quit. Others drop dead from heatstroke or hypothermia. Sometimes fatigue catches up to Angelika and Barbara, too, when racing in 115-degree weather in Death Valley. They've experienced toenails coming off after hours of rubbing against their running shoes. "Sometimes you cannot wash, rinse, or use a decent bathroom for days," they explain.

Despite all that, the twins have won first and second place in many of these survival races, each of them alternately taking the lead. Among other victories, the twins secured gold

 Barbara (on the left) and Angelika receive a trophy at the end of one of the many races they won as a team.

medals at X Games USA and Adventure Race, an invitational hosted by ESPN TV in 1996, and the world record at the 2001 Triple Ironman Triathlon, where they were the first two-woman team to complete the Race Across America, from Oregon to Florida, in nine days and thirteen hours. They were also the first two-woman team in the Alaska Wilderness Classic, which consists of a 350-mile foot race and a small-raft race from Homer to Hope, in 1997. They were both nominated All-American triathletes every year from 1990 to 1997.

On an ordinary Sunday, Barbara rides her bike up and down the neighboring hills for six hours and swims for another two. That's because she's training for Race Across America, but also because it makes her feel good. Training has become the mainstay of the twins' lives; it's what keeps them strong and positive when they're facing other daily obstacles. Twice

33

a week they go canoeing. Twice a week they go climbing. Every other day they set their alarms for 5:00 AM, kissing their warm blankets goodbye and plunging into the pool while the sun is still asleep. They ride their mountain bikes up canyon roads. If it's raining, they go to the gym to pump iron and run on the treadmill. They train for four hours every day. That's what it takes to compete in races like the Ironman: 7 miles of swimming, 78 of running, 336 of biking. This is the regimen they have to maintain if they want to survive the 320 miles of putrid swamps and rocky, steep mountains that make up the X Games trail from Maine to Rhode Island.

The twins must have trained bodies as well as trained minds, since their survival often depends upon making the right decision on the spot. They must know how their bodies will respond to any circumstances, and they must know their strengths and weaknesses to avoid costly mistakes. It's a life-style that calls for self-discipline and organization.

"It's a science," says Angelika. "No room allowed for casualty." Tom Warren, a famous triathlete himself, is a big help to the twins; he has been their coach ever since they started racing, and he has since become Barbara's second husband. He's a contented man, retired and happy, tending to their garden and nurturing the organic produce necessary for the healthy diet they all follow.

Tom is happy to tend to the twins as well, keeping them on track and providing the extra support they need, which nourishes his pride and fosters the twins' self-esteem. "Tom is great," Angelika expresses. "He's not the typical bossy, macho man I've seemed to fall for all my life. Barbara has been much wiser. In marrying him, she won the lottery. Here's a man who's a companion, a good father to his stepkids, and a great coach. I never even imagined men like this existed until I met Tom. And now he's taken, but since my sister is the winner, in some ways he's my prize, too."

ANGELIKA CASTANEDA & BARBARA WARREN

Tom is the one who keeps the twins' schedule, setting the amount of sleep and food they should get or determining when they should go for a massage or a yoga class just to relax. It's not easy to keep a body in shape when it's already seen fifty-plus years. The twins' diet, for instance, has to be strictly maintained. Despite their slender body type, they can't skip one step of their exacting regimen. They need to eat and drink up to six thousand calories a day, divided into six meals at regular intervals. Only monosaturated fats: a few walnuts, avocado slices, and a couple of teaspoons of olive oil. Whole grains only. And pounds of protein. Very little fruit, since it is still sugar, but lots of veggies. "And on top of all that," Angelika adds, "so many vitamins and supplements that we would already be broke, were we not sponsored by a health food company that provides us free goodies."

Never a shake or a candy bar; never a slice of apple pie or a fry. Thinking about that, I imagine that it must have been near impossible with teenagers in the house. "It got easier once the kids were on their own," Barbara confides when I ask her about it. "But temptation is still there, once in a while." A trained body still needs to be happy. As one ages, one tends to indulge a little more. So the twins invented their own creative solution to enjoy life a little more without compromising their efforts. They splurge from time to time when they take short trips out of town. They meet for lunch at some sinful restaurant they fantasize about for days, savoring the pleasure in advance. Just the two of them. What a delight, those couple of hours stolen from their busy schedules, dedicated to relishing yet another of life's flavors, despite its limited access.

Little tricks and creative solutions are women's magic. Women are like alchemists who can cook a potion to cope with any life situation. Being a sports champion is not always easy when you also want to be a champ mom for your kids. It's difficult to want to be there for them, to make them feel comforted by a mother's eternal support, and yet be unable to be there all the time. When her kids were little, Angelika made a point of reassuring her children that she, the unbeatable athlete, was first and foremost their ever-loving mom. As a single mom, she had a live-in babysitter to help her out. The babysitter woke up the kids when Angelika was already out training in the early morning. The babysitter made sure they brushed their teeth, combed their hair, and wore clean clothes. She was the one who made sure they ate breakfast before sending them out to the school bus. But when the kids came home from school, no matter what, Angelika was there. There was no appointment, no commitment more important than the standing one she had with her children every afternoon.

Angelika recalls her sister's help as she was raising her young sons. "Barbara, the psychologist, suggested that my kids, her nephews, needed reassurance. They had to be reminded that they were still a priority in my life so that they wouldn't miss me too much when I was gone. My sister did not have the same problem, since her daughters were grown up by then. She was worried for my children, though. She's always been a great aunt and a big help for a single mom like me. She can feel how I feel, even if she's not in my shoes. She could even feel the pain of my contractions when I was getting ready to give birth."

Such is the intense physical and emotional bond of twins. They are two, but in many ways they are also one. Much more so than married couples or regular siblings, they're bonded beyond blood or will. They are indeed twin souls, twin angels, as no other partners could ever be, embodying the sentiments of Swedenborg, noted seventeenth-century spiritual explorer, when he wrote, "Heavenly wedding is the joining of two in one only mind."

One mind. One heart. Two faces, similar but slightly different. Face to face, identical yet not exactly the same. Angelika speculates that "twins are special from birth. They attract attention. Transforming this attention into fuel to achieve our goals is the peculiar wisdom that we have had to learn. That is the wisdom we would now like to share. Our experience can help every woman, not only twin sisters like us. Sharing has become a huge priority at this time in our lives. There are still a few records to set, still a few mountains to climb. But passing on to others what we consider our own special skill is number one on our list of goals."

The twins' greatest skill is demonstrating the might of their will power. That's the daily lesson their extreme adventures have taught them. That's what Angelika showed the whole world in 1996 on that mountain. Injured but not defeated. Wounded but not powerless. Fallen but still able to get up. Crying with pain and determined to look up. Gritting her teeth and forcing her body to push more, one step after the other, slow but implacable. I've seen the twins in good times and bad times. I've seen them gleaming with satisfaction and overshadowed by disappointment. I've never once seen them complain or feel discouraged for more than a brief moment. They live up to their motto: "By going to the extreme, we bring back lessons for daily living."

They have gone beyond the horizon they saw from the windows of their childhood home. Indeed, they have gone far beyond what even they ever imagined possible.

EPILOGUE

Angelika and Barbara are still as active as ever. When I contacted them to update this chapter, Barbara had just won—once again—the Hawaii Ironman in March 2005. Angelika, meanwhile, had even sweeter news to report: She had gotten

37

married again, just before her sixtieth birthday, to an incredibly charming man. "We have the same interests and like the same things," she told me on the phone. "Preston loves traveling and sports, and he's good to my boys. We've built a house together in Del Mar, and I'm finally happy in my private life as well as my professional life." She invited me to come visit, and I can't wait to take her up on the invitation and reunite with the twins.

When you look back at where you've been, you see how far you've traveled. I don't think anything is a wasted effort.

Ambassador of Women Bikers

GEVIN FAX

A stunning and slender ebony-skinned woman is singing the national anthem during the opening ceremony at the Harley Women's Rodeo, one of several events during the Black Hills Classic in Sturgis, South Dakota. Her voice is angelic, her look pure biker. She wears her hair in long black dreadlocks. She has doe eyes, and her bare skin, tightly wound around solid biceps, shines brightly. Her outfit includes snakeskin leather cowboy boots and a low-cut, black leather strapless corset that reveals a flat bare midriff. Three feet of metal chain encircle her hips in a makeshift belt. A fringed vest, black latex tights, and studded cowboy chaps round out the ensemble. At her feet onstage is a rock 'n' roll acoustic guitar that won't be used in her current performance.

39

"Who's she?" I ask the woman sitting next to me.

"You don't know who that is? She's Gevin Fax. She rocks!" And rock she does. It's 1990, and I've landed in Sturgis, South Dakota, to cover the annual Harley Women Parade for *King,* an Italian magazine. It's my first time at the rally in Sturgis, and this is definitely my first glimpse of this special woman. I will see her again and again, though, several times during this week, performing heavy metal and hard rock tunes onstage. Each time she is dazzling.

She's a biker. She's a rock star. She's a woman of color. She's kick-ass. She's a babe. And most amazingly, she manages to gracefully rise above each of these stereotypes. There is something absolutely unique and genuine about her. She's her own woman, with no need to fit into any prepackaged category. I will not get to know her well until many years later. But I still remember the thrill she gave me the first time I laid eyes on her.

Six years after that first close-up, it's 1996 and I'm in Sturgis once again. I am here of my own accord this time, here to enjoy the Harley-Davidson rally, where bikers from all over the United States have gathered since 1938. For a week they take over this little, otherwise sleepy Midwestern town that sits at the north end of the Black Hills sacred to the Lakota-Sioux Indians. They roam its streets on their loud bikes. They "invade" every bar and restaurant within a fifty-mile radius, performing improv karaoke on any stage they can find, creating stages where they can't find one. They holler from one table to the next, across the room, chatting and laughing with all their friends, old and new.

They set up shop on public streets, erecting dozens of booths where anyone can shop for a tattoo, a skull-and-crossbones bandanna, or the ultimate windproof biker gear. They set up

40

camp just outside of town. They drink hard, party hard, and "live hard," savoring every bit and every taste of this week-long carnival. Many of them will go back to quite a different life: married with children, earning a living at some Joe Schmoe job. But this weekend, their still-long yet graying hair flies in the wind as they ride their bikes around town. They still roam and roar. They act tough, trying to embody the myth of the free spirit. They worship their bikes, taking care of them as if they were their own children.

Time is the ultimate reality check for aging, once-we-were-road-warriors bikers who may have once belonged to the Hell's Angels or another gang. But the crowd that gathers in Sturgis is not the same tribe that used to give housewives the creeps when they'd come to town. The bikers I chat up this weekend can't be the same men who once instilled in mothers the fear that their teenage daughters would be snatched up and swayed by the allure of life on the road. Yet it's obvious that things have certainly changed. With a single glance, upon entering the Buffalo Chip Campground, five miles out of town on a lone country road, it's clear that the bygone days must have indeed been wild ones.

This used to be the craziest, naughtiest camp, the one with the worst bad-bad-boy and bad-bad-girl reputation. Yes, the contest for Miss Wet T-Shirt is still the night's main event, but it's not enough to divert my attention from the staggering number of RVs that I'm noticing this year. I look at the plates, and I'm amazed by the fact that they seem to come from every state, from Idaho to Maryland. The fancy gadgets and thoroughly polished bikes are a sight to behold. These are hard-core bikers who keep their bikes well stored inside their RVs, waiting to show them off during the week's numerous parades before packing them back up to spend the rest of the year at home in the garage.

I marvel at the display in the RV camp: battery-operated

41

television sets that baby-sit the children during long driving hours and restless evenings. Evening card games played on foldable tables take place under awnings to avoid the mosquitoes. Moms wonder whether they'll be able to fit into the same black fringed-and-studded leather corsets that were all the rage twenty years and twenty pounds ago, while dads worry about how they'll be able to handle the sleep deprivation and beer indulgence that never used to slow them down.

Another distraction is the oncoming noise of five hundred bikes coming back into town after a high-speed ride in the hills, simultaneously shifting gears to slow down before hitting the city streets. The decibel level rivals a heavy metal band playing full blast in an enclosed stadium. The forty thousand people who line the streets are as jazzed as concert-goers. In this atmosphere, electrified as if hit by multiple lightning bolts, the arrival of four women bikers may seem like it wouldn't be big news. But when two vans hover in the background with tripods and cameras atop their roofs and production banners announcing the presence of something worthy of television coverage, people stand up and take notice.

Leading the pack of four is the same devilish angel I saw performing six years ago. Radiant and focused yet relaxed, Ms. Gevin Fax projects sheer confidence. She's the type of woman who inspires awe, and I'm hooked. I'll have to investigate more. I'm determined to not let her pass again. She's like a shooting star that I've caught a glimpse of one too many times. Now I need to talk to her.

Gevin is the core of the "cast" for a documentary that Turner Original Productions and Deep River Productions are shooting. The crews have followed Gevin and the other three women on the road for fifteen hundred miles—from the start of their pilgrimage in Los Angeles, California. Gevin's riding companions are Jamie, a journalist married to actor Perry

42

Gevin rides to Sturgis, South Dakota,
during the filming of the TBS documentary
Biker Women.

King; Gail, a photographer and mother of a teenage son; and Cris, a writer and mother of three.

But *Biker Women*—as the documentary was titled when it aired on August 25, 1996, to what turned out to be three million viewers—represents much more than these magnificent four. Women riders, who now comprise 15 percent of the total number of bikers, refuse to ride on the backs of their boyfriends' motorcycles. They want the feel of the open road and the thrill of the ride all to themselves.

Women riders are not trophy passengers. They ride and drive. They take command. They choose their own speed and route. Among them are also a handful of movie stars, including Goldie Hawn, Demi Moore, Bette Midler, Michelle Pfeiffer, Courteney Cox, Cher, Julia Roberts, Ann-Margret, Priscilla Presley, and others. Gevin Fax knows them all. In fact, Gevin owns a detail shop back home in Los Angeles, a "little hole in the Malibu Hills," as she affectionately refers

43

Ambassador of Women Bikers

to it. The whole of show business brings their bikes to The Ladies' Touch Motorcycle Detailing for maintenance and for the tasteful, customizing touches that are Gevin's specialty.

"And it's not just a maintenance shop!" Gevin will specify when we meet for lunch back in Malibu after the festival is over. "I'm also a great instructor. I can teach anybody how to drive in only ten hours. Women are the fastest learners. Harley-Davidsons are my favorite; they're great lady bikes because their center of gravity is so low and close to the ground. It's easy to keep them balanced. They're not so heavy as to require huge pecs and bicep strength. They seem designed for the female body, stronger in the lower part."

Truth be told, Gevin's shoulders, chest, and arm muscles are as solid as her quadriceps and abs. How she's able to find the time to keep in shape, considering that she also holds a nine-to-five day job as a security guard at Malibu High School, is a secret she happily reveals. "I work hard for this body!" she laughs. "I get up every morning at 4:30 and hit the gym, where I indulge myself for two hours. My morning cup of coffee is two hundred sit-ups. And I don't just do it because of how it makes me look. It's more about how it makes me feel. I feel stronger and better when I work out regularly. I have the energy to do everything I love to do. And I love to participate in every part of the things I love to do, some of which require a lot of physical strength.

"I appreciate the opportunities my day job gives me. It's not only the security of a paycheck, a little safety net for a single woman like me who would otherwise probably be a starving artist. Working in a high school provides me the enjoyment of being surrounded by teenagers every day, sharing their enthusiasm, their contagious vital force. I'm like their big sister. They trust me and seek my advice. They ask

44

me questions they can't ask their teachers and don't ask their parents. I could have been one of their teachers if the California school system would accept education degrees from other states. I received mine in Ohio. But in California, my Bachelor of Arts degree is in toilet paper. I should go back to school here to get a California credential, but I never find the time. I already have too many careers!"

She does indeed. On top of her day job, she is also a professional performer, a model-actress, a motorcycle instructor and mechanic, and one of the ambassadors of the Harley Women. "If I want something, I go for it all out. All my life—even when I was a child—I swore that I would never look back and say, 'I wish I had that when I was younger.' I was blessed with the parents I have," she notes. "All of the successes, the medals, the achievements, and everything I am, have stemmed from my parents. When I was little, my recurring nightmare was that I would wake up in someone else's family. Mine was probably the closest thing to the Cosbys you'll ever find."

Gevin's smile is constant. Whether she's talking about her past, present, or future, she's got the glow of a kid who has just dipped her fingers in a candy jar. She's tough but sweet, like jalapeño jam. "When the kids at my school or my concerts ask me who's my hero, I always tell them it's my father. He has a small business as a painter, but he should be a Zen master. He always told my brothers and me, 'Never say *can't*; you can do anything if you are determined to fight for what you want and willing to make the sacrifices to get there.' He has the most positive, optimistic attitude. I've watched him persevere through things that most people would give up on. 'Oh well,' he'd say if he make a mistake or life let him down, 'let's turn the page, forget about the past, move forward, and think about what we can do to prevent this in the future.'"

45

Gevin's mom, a registered nurse, was as inspiring and encouraging as her dad. She taught her daughter to sing.

"But she wanted me to study piano. I wanted to play guitar. So my dad stepped in and said, 'We're not going to spend a bunch of money to give her piano lessons that she'll hate.' He bought me my first guitar, and I started playing in church. I began performing as a solo guitarist at Mad River Mountain ski resort when I was fifteen. I kept playing in nightclubs all over Ohio and supported myself through college with my music."

Before Ohio, however, there was California. Gevin was born Theresa Wallace in Los Angeles. She grew up in Long Beach, where she attended Catholic school. In junior high, she was also known as "Bambi" for those doe eyes of hers. By the time she was fifteen, her father and mother decided to take her two younger brothers and her away from the increasingly dangerous grounds of California high schools.

"My parents had concerns. They didn't want us to be exposed to drugs and guns," Gevin explains. "We moved to my father's home state of Ohio, to Mansfield, a town with a population of five hundred—cats, dogs, and chickens included. The school was so rural that the farmers' children were let out to help during harvest season. My dad tried to sugarcoat it for us. He showed me my room in our new house with its immaculate walls and told me, 'This is your space. You can do whatever you want with it. You can write or draw on the walls, paint them whatever color you want. Whatever makes you feel happy and free. Whatever satisfies your creativity.'"

Gevin's creativity and energy, even then, needed several different outlets. When she announced that she was going to stay out late at night to perform in clubs, her parents did not object. When she bought her first Harley, a 1982 Wideglide, they thought it was dangerous. Yet when Gevin replied, "I'd rather die living than live dying," the case was closed. They were well aware that little Gevin's longtime dream had been to become "a rock star on a sparkling bike."

46

GEVIN FAX

Later on, she was a walk-on for the basketball and track teams at Ohio State University in Columbus. She stayed at OSU for two years but decided that she wasn't getting the academic training that she had expected, so she transferred to Otterbein College in Westerville, Ohio. "There I learned discipline," she acknowledges. In fact, despite her hectic schedule of varsity sports and performing, she was motivated enough to get her degree within four years. "I didn't want to fall behind. Besides, I was paying for my own education."

She received her Bachelor of Arts degree in 1979 with a major in education and a minor in psychology. That same year, her younger brother graduated from high school. The rest of the family moved back to California, but Gevin stayed behind. She had just been hired as a ski instructor at Mad River Mountain. Another temporary job followed at a transportation research center, where Gevin worked as a motorcycle test rider/mechanic. Then she landed an entry-level position with one of Ohio's biggest corporations, United Telephone Company.

"I started to climb the ladder, and pretty soon I was a top manager. They told me early on that I should never expect to achieve the position that I ultimately did achieve. I took it as a challenge. I recalled what my dad had taught me, and I felt like it was my duty to prove them wrong. I heard their naysaying as, 'You can't do this, you'll never amount to anything, you're just not smart enough,' to which I replied through my actions, 'Just watch me.' Only when I finally overcame all my adversaries, gaining their respect on top of it, was I free to go in my mind. I got a big promotion and a raise. I had a fat paycheck and a three-bedroom house on six acres in the countryside. I was also engaged, well on my way to getting married. The problem was, after ten years in management, my job and the prospect of such a structured life no longer made me happy."

47

That problem became serious, and a change more unavoidable, when Gevin, despite the fact that she still lived in Ohio, was exposed to the New Age trend that had originated on the West Coast and was spreading around the country in the 1980s. "I was taking full advantage of all the courses that the company sent me to. When it comes to free education, I'm always first in line. I know there is a whole wealth of knowledge out there, and education is so expensive. One day I attended a seminar that shocked me out of my denial. The seminar leaders told us all, 'You are the master of your own destiny,' then asked the classic question, 'If money were no object, if you could do anything you wanted to, where would you see yourself five years from now?'"

Gevin already knew her answer and had been dreaming about it for a long time, silencing it because of her eagerness to please others and her desire to prove herself. "I realized all of a sudden that I had to fulfill the answer to that question for myself. I wanted to go to Europe, meet new people, sing and play my guitar in front of crowds of fifty thousand people. I wanted to experience the thrill of it. I knew I could never achieve that in Ohio. And so I asked myself what I was still doing there. Many of my coworkers, who had been at United Telephone for thirty-plus years, had never been outside of Ohio. Was I willing to sacrifice the things I had in order to not follow in their footsteps? You bet!"

Although Gevin felt ready, it still took two more years for her to leave Ohio for good. "I quit my job, but I still felt that I'd won the battle but lost the war. I'd spent so much time proving a point to myself. I'd proved that I could do anything, even if it wasn't my thing, and that I wasn't going to let anyone stop me, whatever the cost. But the stress level made me ask, 'Is it really worth proving?'"

But, as always, there was a silver lining. The whole corporate experience had made her stronger. "I think it enabled me

48

to believe that I could survive anything. Everything I learned from what I thought was a waste of time, I used later to pursue my dreams. In the corporate environment, I learned how to be diplomatic and organized, how to dress and act appropriately, how to handle conflict and compliments. I also learned to accept that certain things might never change, no matter how much I bang my head against the wall."

Gevin looks reflective, her usually bright face dimmed, as if seeing a reflection of herself during her corporate time. I wish I could follow her there, since it's impossible for me to picture her in a business suit or career dress, her hair probably relaxed, glossed, styled, and imprisoned by a more "professional" look. "When you look back at where you've been," she interrupts her trance, "you see how far you've traveled. I don't think anything's a wasted effort."

Gevin is a good sport. She learned how to be a team player during her time on college sports teams, and she's always ready to recognize the help she received from others. "When you play varsity sports, you have to rely on your teammates; you can't pull the load by yourself. Women get the same positive reinforcement from sports that men do, and they also need sports as a stress outlet. But I think that men enjoy team sports more because it's the only time society allows them to show affection toward one another. You see these big guys—football players—jumping and holding each other because they made a touchdown. When else do you see that in America? Women are more at ease expressing their emotions and their camaraderie because they don't get immediately labeled. I love playing sports with women as much as I love working toward some creative goal with them.

"The person who supported me the most through everything in Ohio was my personal manager and very good

49

friend, Starr Sutherland-Johnson. She believed in my talent and moved to California with me. She's my partner in the detail shop as well. My family has always supported me, but it's important to also have friends who nurture positive feelings. And in Los Angeles, a city that doesn't present too many opportunities for community feeling, having your own support system can make all the difference."

Starr helped Gevin get her career as a performer going. "My main instrument is now the bass guitar," says Gevin. "I formed an all-woman three-piece band, which is highly unusual and hard to pull off. We called it Galadriel."

Gevin was a big fan of J. R. R. Tolkien long before the *Lord of the Rings* saga was rediscovered. Galadriel was the high lady of the elves in his books, the grandmother of Arwen Undomiel, played by Liv Tyler in the recent movie trilogy. Gevin was also drawn to the notable white horse named Shadowfax that appears in Tolkien's work.

"I would describe myself as a free, wild stallion that loves to run in the wind," Gevin says, "but since there was already a band named Shadowfax, I shortened it to Fax and chose it as my artistic surname." Her new first name, Gevin, was given to her by her brother, David Michael Wallace, who had become a model-actor himself.

"Galadriel was not going to be a group of girls who just shook their behinds in front of men to get ahead. We were good, and we were going to show the world. We played precision rock 'n' roll tunes, particularly those that women traditionally did not play, by bands like Heart, Led Zeppelin, Rush, and a lot of Ronnie James Dio. Very hard rock geared more toward the male crowd. Women usually like it less, but those of us in the band liked it a whole bunch.

"I was living in Mansfield, and so was the drummer. The guitar player lived a good hour away, in Akron. Distance was not an obstacle. We still met to practice three times a week.

50

It was just so energizing that no one ever missed practice. The chemistry between us was unbelievable. I can still recall the emotion of our first performance. There was a crowd and everybody was standing. We knocked their socks off."

After that mesmerizing experience, Galadriel was catapulted into a new realm. "We played huge venues in Cleveland, Cincinnati, and Columbus. We got a lot of recognition from promoters, but they all told us the same thing: 'You girls are ready to move on, and you're not going to go anywhere unless you move to California.' That was kind of a shock. My other two band members weren't really ready to give up their good jobs and nice houses to dive into the unknown. I was, though."

It was the end of Galadriel as they knew it. Without reservation, Gevin went to California without her other two band members. She went with Starr, her manager and supporter, who, like Gevin, was also ready to take control of her own future. And, as often results from some act of pure boldness, opportunity arose; as soon as Gevin and Starr reached California, they got a promising offer.

"I was asked to join a national act, Klymaxx, which had a gold record in 1986. I couldn't believe how well it was going. I was on *Soul Train* and sang background vocals on their album *The Maxx Is Back*. I also performed in two of their videos. I wish I could have shared my luck with my Galadriel companions, but as that seminar leader said, everyone is the master of her own destiny. I just want them to know that I achieved what I set out to do, that it can be done," Gevin adds.

"I think I was meant to perform, and rock 'n' roll was my path. People are often surprised because it's highly unusual to see a black woman who is interested primarily in rock 'n' roll, rather than funk or pop. That was why my allegiance to Klymaxx was fated to be just a stepping stone. It was good

51

Ambassador of Women Bikers

material, but my first love is not funk. I was determined, though, to not give up the feeling of being cheered on by a big crowd.

"The roar of any crowd is one of the most stimulating things a human being can ever experience, whether she's a performer or an athlete or any other kind of competitor. I won some gold medals on the track team, and that feeling of being on the top tier of that podium, when they put those medals around your neck and everybody in the stands cheers for you, is irreplaceable. Or the noise from the stands when you're competing in the race and you hear the encouraging crowd shouting your name. I've always loved competing. I think I will compete—at least within my own limits—until my very last day.

"Athletics also made me a high achiever. Originally, I went to college not so much for the education as to play basketball for four more years. As a woman, even a star athlete, my athletic career would have ended when I graduated from high school. That would have been unbearable for me.

"All I wanted was music, sports, and motorcycles. Even now, if I had money for toys, I'd buy some nice vintage Harleys, a convertible car, a jet ski, and some horses. I cycle, ride horses, run, speed-walk, and water- and jet-ski. I exercise every day, or I get cranky. But more important than anything else is the music. I want to be the first black female rock-'n'-roller to break out another Hendrix revolution. But I also want people to know that I'm for real, and that I didn't get here using drugs.

"I don't even drink alcohol. Can you imagine: a rock-'n'-roller, a biker, and a health nut? A performer who doesn't party and usually goes to bed at nine o'clock so she can get enough rest to work out early in the morning? Well, that's who I am. I have to admit, though, sometimes I have to play it different. When I find myself in a bar in Sturgis, surrounded by drunken bikers who want to buy me a drink, I don't give them attitude.

52

I order a 'Gevin,' a virgin cocktail the bartenders around there named after me. It's made with cranberry and pineapple juice with a bit of tonic, served up in a martini glass with an olive on top. It does the trick, and everybody's happy!

"I'm not afraid of standing my ground to support my convictions, but I learned long ago to avoid conflict unless there is no other choice. Conflict with drunken bikers is not recommended. I have better things to do."

At the same time, Gevin thinks she's never had troubles, not even with the Hell's Angels, because she shows no fear. "Fear is the first baggage a woman needs to get rid of before marching into unknown adventures. When I'm on the road, I put a smile on my face, and I respect, to a certain degree, other people's choices. As long as nobody intimidates or harms anybody in front of me, I mind my own business and am left alone.

"I want to have the freedom of just jumping on my bike and going alone with the wind and the road whenever I feel like it. There's nothing else that gives me such reassurance. It builds my confidence and my instinctive trust in the beauty of our universe. Riding my bike is my therapy. It calms me down better than yoga. When I'm keyed up, the best thing is to go out on the highway and ride. I don't believe in Prozac or in sleeping pills; I believe in riding my Harley. I can ride up to eight or nine hours. Sometimes even that's not enough.

"When we were very little, my father took us mini-bike and go-kart racing. Then he bought an Italian Mobilette moped before they were introduced in the United States. From then on I was addicted. My younger brother and I would ride everywhere on the Ohio streets. We'd pack a lunch in a backpack and leave at sunrise, telling Mom and Dad we were going exploring. We'd end up sixty miles from home, savoring the independence as much as our peanut butter sandwiches."

Gevin credits her Harley for getting her most of her

53

California connections. "As soon as I hit Los Angeles from Ohio, I rode to Hollywood Boulevard. I sat down where all the bikers were. I introduced myself and asked questions. Bikers are one of the modern American tribes. Compared to others—surfers for instance, who are much stricter about their acceptance rules—bikers are very open and supportive with each other.

"They told me where the motorcycle gatherings were and what nights the promoters came out. Soon I got an audition for a Harley-Davidson commercial. As soon as it came out, I'd ride on the boulevard, and people would say, 'Oh, that's the woman who was in the heavy metal band. She plays music and sings.' So it helped my music, too."

If biking is her therapy, music is Gevin's child. "I'm not kidding," she insists. "I have been so focused on my career as a performer that I've ruled out having a husband and babies. My music is my husband and my child. It's my obsession!" It's also her only recreational drug, coupled with adrenaline. "The first time I experienced that kind of 'shake' as a musician, I was the only soloist asked to perform at the Columbus Battle of the Bands. Everyone else had four-, five-, and six-piece bands—hard rock or heavy metal. It was great music, and the crowd enjoyed it, but they kept yelling between songs, 'Play some Neil Young!'"

The more she gets into the moment, the more Gevin's eyes darken and brighten with excitement. If coffee could sparkle, her eyes would be two cupfuls. "Let's say it," she laughs, "I was scared to death. It was the first time I had played to a packed house. The lights were so bright that I couldn't really see farther than the first two rows. But I could feel the rush in the air when the crowd cheered. The fourth band finished, and I thought, 'Oh God!' There was this hush . . . I dragged my stool across the floor, and I could hear the squeak.

"I finally got situated, put my acoustic guitar on my lap,

and looked up. 'I understand you want some Neil Young,' I said. I felt like Charlie Brown getting blown off the pitcher's mound. I had to check if my shoes were still on! I broke out with two Neil Young tunes, then five more. I was the only performer who got a standing ovation that night. I couldn't believe people would enjoy the music I played that much. It was so beautiful that I almost cried. That's the magic of music or, I guess, of performing: You feel so good making others feel good.

"I can't bear performers who do rotten shows in front of worshipful crowds because they're so drunk or stoned that they don't care. I think fans are due the utmost respect. People pay good money to see a performance. When a performer doesn't care about the audience, that's very insulting. In my opinion, you owe them; they put you there where you stand."

There were two other memorable times when Gevin felt the power of the crowd. The first was when Galadriel performed at the Cleveland Riverfest. The other was when she debuted in Hollywood with the heavy metal band Boetto. "'Boetto! Boetto!' the crowd was cheering, over and over," Gevin recalls. "Again, I was almost scared. I realized the power in that crowd could tear me apart just to get a piece of me. And yet I was in heaven."

Gevin didn't play many shows with Boetto, however; it's a hardcore, instrument-heavy band, whereas Gevin is at her best with melodic hard rock with vocals. "Nevertheless, they're the greatest group of guys I've had the good fortune to work with. I still collaborate sometimes with guitarist Tom Taggert, who's a musical child prodigy, so young and just so good. He can play every instrument, and he's the sweetest young man."

Tom is one of the few men in her life, besides her brother

55

and father, who have supported Gevin through good and hard times, and with whom she has a lasting friendship.

"I have more women than men friends. Maybe it's because women have less pretenses. They're not so needy and they give more. With a life as full as mine, I can't afford to drag any heavy weight. Most men tend to bend in front of a strong woman. And I don't want to depend on anybody, but I also don't want anybody to depend totally on me. Who knows? Maybe one day I'll find a real match. Until that day, I'd rather roam happily single."

EPILOGUE

I met Gevin again several times over the years. Whether it was a women's bike ride or a concert, a marathon or a spiritual ceremony, she was always game to hang out.

Then, between my many moves and hers, we lost track of each other. Just when I was starting to write this book, I found Gevin's website. I was pleased to see that she's still doing everything she wants to do and everything she lives for. And she looks as happy and energetic as I remember her being the first time I spotted her, almost fifteen years ago.

"I was injured doing a stunt for the movie *Catwoman,* so I've been on disability for a while," she tells me when we finally talk again after several years. "But I used my recovery time to work on a feature film on bikers with my buddies from *Biker Women.* The working title is *Chopper Shop.* The director is Gayle De Marco, and the producer is Chris Sommers. Willie Nelson is in it, and we're hoping to cast Ann-Margret!"

Since she's been in California, Gevin has appeared in a segment of the TV show *America's Most Wanted* and in a few movies, *Pork* and *The Venus Machine* among them.

Since the last time we spoke, she bought her first house in the Los Angeles area and a cabin in Los Padres National

Forest. She's taken some time off from her job as a security guard for Malibu High since her injury, but she's planning on going back full-time once she's completely healed.

One makes the difference. Yes, even only one. I always stood up for what I believed in, even as a kid.

Compassionate Environmentalist

✦ ✦ ✦

JULIA BUTTERFLY HILL

She's having a party for her twenty-fourth birthday on top of the world, or at least at one hundred eighty feet off the ground. Only there will be no guests, just birthday cards and cellular phone greetings. She'll be dancing all alone up there, as she has done for almost three months, every other day, on good days. She'll drink organic zinfandel and splurge on a vegan carrot cake. She'll dream of a hot shower, the luxury she misses the most.

Julia Butterfly Hill is neither an astronaut orbiting the earth nor a hermit. She's a poet. And where better for a poet to live than at the top of a giant, one-thousand-year-old tree named Luna? This redwood in Humboldt County is Julia's new mailing and residential address; she will ultimately spend 738 days in her tree house in an act of protest. "Butterfly," too, is a name she's adopted around the time I meet her in early 1998. It's her "forest name," the one she assumed when she entered the activist world in Northern California. It wasn't hers—yet—when she was born in Arkansas, the eldest daughter of a traveling evangelist. "I really am the daughter of a preacher through and through, after all," she later reveals in her memoir, in an attempt to explain why anyone in their right mind would take up residence in a tree for two years.

When we meet in February 1998, Julia has been sitting in her newfound dwelling in stormy Humboldt County under a wall of rain for almost a hundred days. El Niño storms ravage the forest, every week a bit worse than the previous one. It is one of the coldest and stormiest winters on record. High winds are roaming the ocean, raising hell with waves up to thirty feet.

This stretch of still-undeveloped California coastline is called the Lost Coast for its rugged beauty, appealing more to nature lovers than to the flocks of tourists who prefer the fancy attractions, such as Disneyland or Hollywood, that Southern California offers. Here, taller than Magic Mountain, stand the tallest trees in the world.

If you happen to enter Grizzly Creek Redwoods State Park and hike up any given trail, you'll soon find yourself surrounded by these awesome redwood giants. Some taller than twenty-story buildings—hundreds of feet high—the redwoods create a forested cathedral more awe inspiring than any European incarnation. In winter, the thick white fog that rolls into Humboldt County and blankets the coastline only reaches the base of their trunks. The average redwood is so large that you could carve a comfortable two-bedroom apartment inside it; it takes ten people holding hands at arms length to embrace its perimeter.

The trees are welcoming. Their musky nests beckon to visitors to pray for their endangered destiny. Only a few hundred are left, but still not few enough for greedy loggers to leave them alone.

Loggers' clear-cutting operations are captained by the local Pacific Lumber/Maxxam Corporation (PLC), which claims ownership of most of the Headwaters Forest, and have been instrumental in the particular severity of the mudslides and damages in 1998. Some Humboldt County residents living in the tiny town of Stafford had their share of troubles the previous winter, when PLC handed them the worst New Year's Eve news they could remember.

On December 31, 1996, they woke up to the thundering sound of the mountain above their homes sliding toward them, trailing a huge wall of capsized redwood and Douglas fir trees, stumps and rocks in tow. One resident compared it to "lava flowing out of an erupting volcano." It had enough force to lift the first house it hit and to hurl a pickup truck into another one parked across the street. The slide carried enough dirt to fill up the entire basin, containing the whole of the town, with eight to seventeen feet of mud and debris.

How did this happen? Stripped of the towering trees that had once lined its surface, the steep slope above the town had nothing to trap the rocks and dirt as they came cascading down. The heavy rains were strong enough to loosen the hillside, liquefying the mountain—and threatening to bury Stafford under its muddy pudding.

And yet just days after the "Stafford accident," the California Department of Forestry approved a plan to clear-cut another slope in the immediate proximity of an impressively ancient redwood tree. That threatened tree would soon be world renowned. Christened Luna (for "moon" in both Spanish and Italian), the behemoth was destined to become Julia Butterfly Hill's new home for the next two years, despite many attempts (both peaceful and violent) by various parties to evict her.

Julia lived alone in the tree most of the time. Sometimes people would come to visit, particularly in the beginning. But as time went on and the platform where Julia lived became increasingly dangerous and frail, she had fewer and fewer visitors, even as support for what she was doing continued to grow. The circle of friends and admirers on the ground expanded day by day as news of Julia's ambitious activities spread quickly. By her twenty-fourth birthday, about three months into her protest, Julia's endeavor had garnered international media attention.

I had heard about Julia's unique cause months earlier and had started trying to pitch a story about her. I knew I had to profile her; her adventurous spirit had captivated my imagination. Here was a young woman doing something unprecedented: She had been sitting in a tree longer than any other tree-sitter before her. She had survived helicopter attacks and horrible weather. She had defeated fear and reached inside herself to find enough humor and love to express kindness instead of bitterness, even toward her aggressors.

Julia's twenty-fourth birthday created an unexpected stir. It's funny how the media works: Suddenly, the *Los Angeles Times, Newsweek,* and *Time*—and seemingly every other newspaper and magazine around the world—decided it was time to write about her to give that catchy story a personal angle. And so it was that when I arrived, I was hardly the first or only writer anxious to talk to Julia about what she was doing.

JULIA BUTTERFLY HILL

I have to climb a mountain in order to see Luna and Julia. I go with a group of people headed by drummer Mickey Hart, best known for his long journey with the Grateful Dead. The hope is that percussions and drumming far below her nest will warm Julia up, even in this damp cold. My hope is that I won't be in Humboldt too long, that I can get home to Los Angeles rather quickly so I can pitch Julia's story to the Italian media and let Italian readers know what's going on up here in this remote and forested wonderland. I'm a storyteller through and through, and telling the stories of people committed to living their truth is what I'm here to do. It's what I'm meant to do.

Julia's story starts with Luna, who was baptized by a handful of activists from Earth First!, self-described as a "direct-action movement started in 1980 by people tired of the failures of trying to work within the political system."

Julia is a great team player who has a mind of her own and who reserves the right to decide on single issues. She is a blend of individualism and the struggle for the greater good. The importance of "togetherness" is a big part of who she is. Julia is very much her own person, and while she is happy to work toward common goals, she does not suffer those who try to dictate the means by which she works to achieve those goals. Her method, after all, proved her to be more effective than any other activist in this field had been prior or since.

In October 1997, upon learning of the logging of an area close to the Stafford slide, Earth First! went to check out the operation. They spotted a huge redwood tree standing atop the hill above the town. The trunk was marked with blue paint, indicating that it was slated for destruction. A few days later, Earth First! returned to the hill, hiking up the trail with ropes and wood scraps recovered from a salvage yard. They built a wooden platform and installed it in the tree's branches, one hundred eighty feet above the ground. That same night, they named her "Luna," taking custody of the magnificent tree as she bathed in the bright light of a full moon.

Sitting at the top of a cliff near the crest of a steep hill gives Luna certain peculiar traits. She can be seen for miles, and she has not grown as straight as most redwoods do. Her trunk measures twelve feet in diameter. Two caves have been carved into the bottom of her trunk, which is also scarred by deep, black marks, an indication that she was once struck by lightning. She survived thanks to the thick, moist bark that not only preserves her but also gives life to other vegetation sprouting from her trunk. If you look closely at the bark, you start to see different shapes and designs.

Her limbs intertwine and create a jungle in the sky. Her foliage is scattered at different heights, all the way up to two hundred feet. At about eighty feet from the ground, the tree splits in two and then rejoins a few feet higher before splitting again into two pillars. Suspended from this new growth is the platform that has become Julia's home. This is best seen from a distance, as discerning Luna's very unique structure from the ground is nearly impossible. One of these two side-by-side parts of the same trunk ends at about a hundred and fifty feet up, and the other shoots skyward, as if reaching for the heavens.

Julia climbed up there for the first time in November 1997, lifting herself with a rudimentary harness held together with duct tape. When she got to the top, she was awed by Luna's power and by the worldview from her perch. A little while later, around the time that I first visited her, Julia would declare that she had made a promise to Luna, and also to Mr. Campbell, the Australian-born president of Pacific Lumber, that she would not descend until the corporation promised to spare the life of this tree that had become a symbol for environmentalists all over the world.

JULIA BUTTERFLY HILL

By the time I arrived, no one was allowed to ascend to the six-by-eight foot platform; stormy winds and rain had made it too fragile, and more weight would have imperiled Julia's own ability to subsist with her few supplies. Visitors could only reach Julia by climbing up a younger, smaller tree that faced Luna from the south, at the same level on the hillside next to her.

The good news is that living in a place as remote as a platform atop a giant redwood is no longer a problem as far as communication is concerned. Julia was equipped with walkie-talkies, a cellular phone, a radio, and a video camera— technology that recently saved her life when she was under helicopter siege during a storm. "I never thought I'd have my hand on the record button of a video camera and my ear glued to a cellular phone as much as I have since I've been up here," she tells me as soon as we start to talk. "And I'm somebody who has never even used a typewriter! One day or another, when we've exhausted the earth's power resources, we'll have to do without all this technology we've been spoiled with and go back to the old ways. But I can certainly appreciate what technology has provided for Luna's and my own sake."

Julia is striking and, at five feet ten inches, very tall. Her natural beauty is accentuated by a wild and grungy look that includes layers upon layers of clothing. Only her smile and her long, untamed hair shows underneath her hat, scarf, wool sweaters, and thermal pants. "Cotton wouldn't do it," she explains. "Cotton becomes icy cold when it gets wet. And it's easy to get dripping wet with sweat when you climb from one branch to the other, as I do most of the day."

Curiously, she's barefoot, despite the chill. "I got rid of my shoes a while ago. It was too difficult to feel whether the branches I was trying to climb to could support my weight. And the rubber soles were a barrier between Luna and me. She couldn't guide me that way; she couldn't help me move safely on her. I started to move around without the harness almost right away for the same reason."

Julia talks about Luna the way an affectionate, respectful young woman would talk about her grandmother. She bows to Luna's wisdom. She asks for and treasures Luna's advice. She turns to Luna for strength and comfort when she's feeling down. There is a spiritual bond between the woman and the tree. They communicate with and understand each other, a magic often missing between human beings.

The bond with the redwoods was immediate, Julia says.

"As soon as I set foot in this forest for the first time, I felt like there was something here I was called to do. It was my first trip after a terrible car accident I had had in Arkansas. One night in August 1996, I was rear-ended by a Ford Bronco. The impact folded my little Honda like an accordion, shoving the back end of the car almost into the back of the driver's seat. The impact was so strong that the stereo burst out of its console and bent the stick shift. I avoided being thrown through the windshield only because I was wearing a seat belt. But my head snapped back into the seat, then slammed forward onto the steering wheel, jamming my right eye forward into my skull.

"I suffered brain damage. It wasn't evident at first, not even through an MRI. But I started losing my ability to move, and I was always falling. It took almost a year of intensive therapy for the information tunnels in my brain to be retrained and rerouted and for my short-term memory and motor skills to return. I made it, despite the skepticism of doctors.

"Perhaps it was because I had injured the left, analytical side of my brain that the right, more creative side started to speak to me and my perspective shifted. I wanted to follow a more spiritual path and find out what I was meant to be and what I needed to do to find my sense of purpose.

"I wanted to go on a journey, and it happened like this:

66

Three of my friends announced that they were setting out on a trip to the West Coast. They had room for a fourth in their car, and I couldn't have been happier to join them. Our plan was to go all the way up to Washington's Olympic Rain Forest, but we met a total stranger on the road who told us we had to stop in Humboldt County and see the Lost Coast and the redwoods. I felt immediately drawn to his idea, and when we arrived at Grizzly Creek Redwoods State Park, I asked my friends to leave me there with my backpack. They wanted to stay only for a short while, but I needed to *be* there for as long as it would take to understand why I felt called by this forest.

"Once alone with the trees, I was swallowed into an energy wave, gripped by the spirit of the forest. I felt the film covering my senses, resulting from the imbalance of years lived in a technologically dependent, fast-paced society, melt away. I could feel my whole being resurrected into a new life in this majestic cathedral."

I immediately relate to what Julia must have experienced. Trees are like some animals: patient, strong, and generous. They're always there to listen and to provide their comforting presence. An Indian friend of mine once offered me a recipe for relieving stress and despair: "Go out and hug a tree," he said. It wasn't some hippie mantra, either. I did just that, and I can testify that it is both connecting and rejuvenating. In fact, I attribute much of my own self-confidence to the perspective I discovered while climbing trees when I was a little girl. Sitting on top of a huge persimmon tree in my grandma's garden made me feel like I could touch the moon, the clouds, and the stars with my little finger. I could share songs with the birds and escape the taunting of my older cousins and sister. Nesting in the tree, I was protected and invincible. And that was only thirty feet off the ground. I can only imagine how Julia feels now, six times higher than that. And I can definitely understand why, after experiencing

67

that rush of energy from the redwoods, she walked out of that forest a different woman.

"A couple of weeks later," continues Julia, "I found out that if I had walked just a few steps more along the path, I would have landed in a clear-cut, courtesy of Pacific Lumber/Maxxam Corporation. I also learned that less than 3 percent of these unique trees were left in the world, the rest of the wood turned into patio furniture and fancy house decks and fences.

"I went back to Arkansas and settled my lawsuit for the car accident. I sold everything I had, except for a few things that had sentimental value and that I stored at my father's house. With the sale money, I bought a new backpack, a sleeping bag, and a tent. I packed just a couple changes of clothes and prepared to return to California to save the redwood forests. I had no clue what I could do, but I knew that I was meant to do something."

The beginning wasn't easy, however. Julia had to learn that activism is much more complicated than just climbing up a tree to announce its right to live. In Julia's neophyte eagerness, she hadn't foreseen the waiting game that is often necessary in putting together effective protest. "It was tough. I knew I was there for a reason, but I was told I wasn't needed. When I reached a base camp in Arcata, a town full of forest activists and students from Humboldt State University, I was told that it was closing. No one seemed to want me there. Most didn't even care to talk to me. But there was one guy, whose name was Shakespeare, who seemed to understand my urgent desire to do something. He told me not to give up and not to be discouraged. He said there were tree-sits going on, and that if I had the strength to stick it out a little longer, he could help get me trained to climb so I could get up one of those trees."

68

Installing human beings around the clock in platforms high in the trees prevents a tree from being cut down and simultaneously draws attention to the necessity of protecting our forests. It is a tactic of peaceful civil disobedience that has proven highly effective.

Shakespeare kept his promise to show Julia the ropes, and Julia did stick it out. Another activist named Almond, whom Julia came to know and appreciate in the following months, was going around camp, asking for volunteers to sit in Luna. Although Julia felt she was inexperienced, she wanted to be part of the tree-sitters team when she saw that only Shakespeare and another guy by the name of Blue had volunteered.

The small group arrived at Luna after an exhausting hike on a muddy, steep path. Julia was shocked. She recounts, "The harness and rope looked so unfit for the purpose: The rope was about the width of a dime, and the harness had duct tape holding it together! But I wanted to go up so bad that in a matter of minutes, I learned how to tie a prussic knot and move it along the rope, and how to secure metal carabiners." Julia's training course lasted a total of three minutes.

"When I started to climb, I was definitely scared. I didn't trust the harness to remain in one piece; I was skeptical about the thinness of the rope. And then I heard Luna's voice for the first time. My attention shifted from the thin rope to her massive trunk, from fear to attention. I simply started to pay more attention to the tree I was climbing, and the fear dissolved . . . for the moment, at least!"

Julia certainly felt her share of fear, even panic. Her first stay in Luna lasted only six days, in the company of her two new friends, Shakespeare and Blue. She learned other skills as quickly as she had learned how to climb, including how to cook and wash dishes with the least possible water and how to sleep completely still so that she would fit under the tarp on the tiny, crowded platform. Rather than getting to know Luna,

69

Compassionate Environmentalist

she spent time getting to know more about her companions and their activist lifestyles. After six days, she descended for a day's respite, only to return and find that Shakespeare and Blue had descended and a new tree-sitter named Mike had taken their place.

"Mike told me about attempts made to physically force him out of a tree-sit with pepper spray. Law enforcement officers swabbed it directly into his eyes so that he would get out of his locked-down position, a common position among sitters that entails locking your legs around a branch so it's really difficult to pull you away. His story filled me with sadness and horror. I didn't have a clue at that point that I would endure a similar threat to my life after Mike left and I was the only person sitting in Luna.

"Mike was also the first to tell me about Earth First!. I asked him what it was. 'It's the group you're part of!' he said. But I wasn't part of any group, and I'm still not. 'Well, they're the ones who started this tree-sit,' he informed me, 'and if you haven't had any nonviolence or backwoods training, that's against the regulations.' I didn't know one needed to be versed in regulations in order to sit in a tree. I had just volunteered because there was nobody else."

As Julia sat with Mike over the next several days, she fell very ill. This was before she was given a cell phone with which to communicate with the outside world.

"I started to feel lightheaded and queasy, with hot and cold flashes and shakes so strong that they sent me into convulsions. It freaked out Mike, and I was freaked out myself. It reminded me of how I had felt after my car accident. Finally, on Thanksgiving Day, Almond showed up with a group of fresh tree-sitters. I was relieved and free to get back to town. It took me almost three weeks to get rid of my illness. It turned out that two different viruses had attacked my system, one of which had started to move into my kidneys."

JULIA BUTTERFLY HILL

While she was nursed back to health by rest and the care of the other activists with whom she was beginning to form friendships, Julia had a chance to closely observe Almond's coordinating job from the ground. She saw how much energy went into moving tree-sitters up and down the hill to Luna, often to sit for only a few days at a time.

"It was chaos, and the cutting was getting closer to Luna every day. The answer to this problem came to me very quickly, and I convinced Almond that the best solution to the organizational problems would be to let me sit in Luna by myself, with enough stuff to keep me going for three weeks to a month.

"Almond agreed to the plan and helped me buy bulk food and spices—I can't stand bland food—and enough water. When we were finally ready, on the evening of December 10, each of us was carrying at least a hundred pounds. We had to hike up at night. In daylight we'd have risked getting arrested for trespassing on Pacific Lumber's property. It took an hour and a half just to harness all our provisions up."

The very next day, Luna endured her first axe attack.

"I could feel the vibrations coming up through her trunk, and I assumed the loggers were going to blow up the tree with Almond and me sitting up in the platform, just as they had threatened they would. Then I spotted Climber Dan in the other tree, and I became paralyzed with terror. He was a Pacific Lumber guy, notorious for his aggression and for removing people from tree-sits.

"Almond got out on a traverse line, and when he was midway across, suspended high above the forest on those two tiny ropes waving back and forth and bending with each step, they confronted each other in a yelling match. Climber Dan threatened to cut the traverse line, even though he could see that Almond wasn't wearing a safety line.

71

Compassionate Environmentalist

"Almond tried to retreat, but he still dropped two and a half feet the moment Climber Dan sliced the rope. It was only because he had retreated as much as he had that his foot caught a big branch that prevented him from falling over one hundred feet to his death. I was shaken by necessity out of my paralysis. Almond had taught me that a tree-sit is also a form of public outreach, and this time we had a cell phone. Stranded on the platform and unable to maneuver around the tree to get more concrete help, I started dialing. There was a list of six different radio stations' and newspapers' numbers on a scrap of paper near the phone, so I started there. I reached radio KZYX but only got an answering machine. In my altered state, I took my chance and left a babbling message anyhow. As I was dialing the second number, Annie Espeziedo from KZYX called me back."

That moment marked the beginning of the transformation from private Julia into public, media-savvy Julia. It was the beginning of her realization that she'd have to share with the media much more than she had ever wished or imagined, including her ingenious schemes for going to the bathroom and getting rid of waste from one hundred eighty feet up in the air.

She would ultimately allow cameras to film her emotions when she cried; she played along with dirty jokes by smartass disc jockeys. She allowed all these requests and probes into her life in order to save Luna and the forest.

"Come on," she teases me, "aren't you dying to know how I go to the bathroom?"

Am I? I definitely am, I conclude—as much as I am also interested in knowing how she keeps her long, thick mane clean and shiny, or how she washes and rinses her body in this freezing climate. Since I'm used to traveling alone in the outdoors and setting up camp along the road, I am actually very interested. I consider the fact that the situations I've been in don't measure up, even by a little bit, compared to what Julia is doing. I have to battle my urge for a good shower, resolving to trade it in for peace and closeness to nature. Would I last more than a few days without a hot shower and a toilet? I have my doubts.

"Human beings are very adaptable" Julia assures me. "We learn out of necessity. We learn out of conviction. Saving Luna was reason enough to learn how to use a bucket for a toilet and how to take two-minute sponge baths in successive intervals, stripping first from the waist up and covering back up, and then from the waist down to maximize warmth. I have to move fast to avoid freezing. I've even learned to dance this way. Sometimes I hold a branch tightly with my legs and dance from the waist up with my arms raised. Sometimes I keep a grip on Luna with my arms and shake my body from the waist down."

Since I'm curious about her grooming habits, she completes her personal hygiene survival lesson for my benefit. "I get rid of the waste by harnessing the bucket down every few days when somebody comes to restore my water, food, or battery supplies. Pretty simple. And I massage my scalp and brush my hair with herbal oil. If you think about it, our great-grandmothers were probably doing the same in certain parts of the world where running water and other comforts did not exist. So I'm not doing anything so special.

"Yet," she laughs, "sometimes I think I look like a monkey up here! I had confirmation of that a little while ago, when I was trying to find a space to better communicate with a Pacific Lumber guy. He was part of Pacific Lumber's 24/7 siege, starting on January 20, to get me down once and for all. As much as I feared and resented the security guards, I also felt bad for them. Charles Hurwitz [the head of Maxxam Corporation]

Julia salutes another day on top of Luna.

should have been the one sitting under the tree in such nasty weather, not them. They sat at the base of the tree, taking turns talking to me. I could see them from where I stood, and sometimes they would climb onto the lower branches so we could communicate without the walkie-talkies.

"I was praying for the guards to be transferred back to their warm trailers as much as I was praying for my own safety. I wanted to interact with them as human beings, not as enemies. I knew they were seeing me as a kind of crazy environmentalist. They couldn't understand why I would want to spend so much time in a tree. So I put some of my granola in a bag, figuring they were probably hungry, and I added one of my prettiest photographs of myself, which had been taken long before I arrived in Humboldt. I lowered it down in my bucket, and one of the guards, Kalani, picked it up.

JULIA BUTTERFLY HILL

"At first he didn't even believe it was me. 'This is not you!' he yelled up to me. But I finally convinced him that if I were to take a shower and style my hair, I would actually start to resemble the girl in that photo. He asked me, 'So if you really look like this, what are you doing all alone in a tree?' His idea was that a pretty girl should have a boyfriend, or else something was probably wrong with her. He figured I should belong to a man, not to a tree. If I was up here, it was probably because I hadn't found the right guy. He resorted to trying to get me down by inviting me to have dinner and sing with the band he was playing with.

"I liked him, though. We started talking. He was keeping me company, and we got to know each other. That's when Pacific Lumber removed him from surveillance, probably thinking that he was getting too much of a soft spot for that dirty, dangerous, anarchistic tree-sitter."

Julia is always thoughtful of others, and that is definitely one of her secret weapons. She tries to see the other people's points of view. She strives for understanding. She can handle confrontation, but her tone remains calm and kind. Julia truly cares, and her amazing grace disorients her enemies, forcing them to look at her from a more human perspective, even when she is under huge stress in the worst possible conditions.

One of Julia's greatest tests of character occurred on January 20, 1998. "In Luna," explains Julia, "the wind is the worst thing to endure. It makes your thoughts go wild. You can't focus, or read or write or paint. You feel disconnected and ungrounded. The sound of the tarps whipping in the air drives you crazy. Your mind gets blown away. Now, imagine knowing that the cause of all this is not just wind from nature, but the wind stirred up by a helicopter hovering no more than a few feet above your head. Try to imagine having to hold onto a branch with all your arm strength to avoid being swept away like a leaf.

"It was the first day the weather finally cleared after days of fog, wind, and rain. When I heard the sound, I thought the helicopters were coming to harvest the many fallen trees on the ground. A logger passing down warned me, 'Come down now or get ready for a really bad hair day!' In a matter of minutes, the helicopter rose from behind the ridge. As it got closer, it got louder and louder. It was heading straight for me.

"If it weren't for the vibration I was starting to feel, I'd have thought I was hallucinating. I kept waiting for the helicopter to swerve. Instead, it continued straight on. Trying to keep myself from panicking, I climbed out as far as I could on a branch to videotape the assault with a camera that had recently been sent up by Earth First!. I filmed the helicopter with my legs wrapped tight under a branch. It wasn't easy.

"The slightest movement could have whipped me down. The stench coming from the burning fuel of this huge, noisy machine just above my head was so disgusting that I started to feel nauseous. The sound was like artillery rounds being fired right in between my ears. I felt like I was on the world's scariest roller coaster, adrenaline pulsing through my pores. It seemed to last forever, even though everything happened in a matter of seconds.

"Pretty soon, the helicopter was gone as quickly as it had come. But I had caught its vicious attack on tape. My friends at Earth First! mailed the tape to the Federal Aviation Administration, and that was the end of their helicopter attacks. It is absolutely against regulations to fly within two hundred feet of humans." After the incident, Julia was contacted by CNN to participate in a debate with John Campbell, the president of Pacific Lumber. Later she arranged to talk to him privately. "He's a tough cookie," Julia laughs. "Pacific Lumber has permission to cut down trees in this area until the year 2000.

JULIA BUTTERFLY HILL

I hope he won't make me stay here to defend Luna for that long. I would if I had to, and he knows that. But I think we're making progress. At least he isn't sending any more helicopters, and at least I've stopped being afraid that I'll die up here. Man, that was scary!"

"I feel so blessed," says Julia with a smile, "to have found people who support me with so much love, taking big risks for my sake. There have been many occasions when there would have been nothing I could have done had it not been for the support of my team. It's like a car race: Somebody is at the steering wheel, and at the finish line the driver gets the trophy and the spotlight. But everybody knows that he had a top-of-the-line car and a top-of-the-line pit crew, that all the bolts were tightened to perfection, and that everything was lubricated just right. The whole team deserves that trophy."

Julia's team included her parents, who supported her struggle in every way they could. As a parent myself, I knew how hard it is for a parent to accept that their own child is doing dangerous things. I really admired Julia's parents when she told me about how they supported her. "My dad would talk to the media, and my mom, who's very religious, would pray with me over the phone when I felt down or scared or exhausted. That gave me so much strength; prayer is an incredible resource, and I get to pray in this incredible natural temple.

"Luna has become my church. She taught me things I didn't know about myself. She has shown me how to remain still, rooted to the earth, even in the eye of the storm. It will be hard to leave her when I go back to the world. But I am sure I'll never go back to my life as it was, or to who I was before."

77

Julia is serene and happy now in the tree.

"Nothing I've done so far even comes close to the satisfaction of what I'm doing now. That doesn't mean I intend to spend the rest of my life hanging from tree branches. But I know that whatever I'll end up doing to make a living, I'll never forget what I learned here in this forest.

"I have seen how new life grows from old life. I've seen how the smallest insect has its own role in the universal balance. I now understand how lucky humans are to be graced with this abundance, and how irresponsible we are acting by destroying it without even a second thought. Money rules many parts of the world, but not for me. I see my life from now on as one of service.

"Awareness has become part of who I am. It has changed everything—the way I breathe, eat, and even love. I always wanted to have children, but now I think I will adopt instead, maybe the older ones, the teenagers nobody wants to take home, afraid that they've been through too much.

"Why do you need to have a child who has your eyes, nose, and mouth? Isn't it enough to have children who will appreciate and follow your values, treasure your affection, and reward you with their smiles? It should be enough, shouldn't it?"

Julia is a dreamer as much as she's a woman of action. She's a pragmatic hermit and a realistic visionary. She can look outside of herself, outside of the society in which she's been raised, and imagine worlds of restored beauty. Yet she is equally able to come down to earth and describe in detail what she will do the day she physically returns to the ground. And she has big plans: "First, I'll take a long, hot shower. Then I'll fill the bathtub with hot water perfumed by salts. I'll light candles and I will drink white wine in a flute."

JULIA BUTTERFLY HILL

When I visited, that day was a far-off possibility, as it would only come if and when Pacific Lumber accepted Julia and Earth First!'s demands, which ask that the loggers limit their cutting to younger trees and stop using harsh chemicals to get rid of weeds, since the chemicals contaminate the soil for many years to come. "We have been very reasonable," Julia says. "We have tried to take the economic interests of the logging corporation into account, but we want them to at least respect the oldest and irreplaceable trees. Luna has more than a thousand years of history hanging on her branches. Shouldn't that weigh heavier than the fifty thousand dollars that her lumber would yield? As soon as they sign the agreement, I will descend."

I'm almost hesitant to ask, but I have to. "What if they won't sign?"

"Then I guess," Julia cracks up, "I'll celebrate my next birthday with the mice and flying squirrels that are visiting me here."

"Now that I can be in touch with everybody in the short time it takes to dial numbers, I don't feel so lonely anymore. I wasn't anyhow. I have a tree as my soul mate. Who needs a boyfriend?"

EPILOGUE

Much of what happened in Julia's life after she descended Luna at the end of October 1999 is well known, as she has continued her promise to be a prominent activist for the many environmental interests she supports.

I got back in touch with Julia in 2005 to ask her what she was up to.

"The work to save the old-growth forests in California and the United States continues," she told me. "We have won some protections, but under the current government, many more areas are being destroyed. We continue to work on all fronts, from direct action to lawsuits to consumer education, to protect and restore our forests."

Julia is the founder of Circle of Life Foundation, an Oakland, California–based group. "Circle of Life is dedicated to helping people find their own version of 'their tree' in the world," Julia explains. "What this means is that we help people connect with the ways they can make a difference in the world. For me, service is about living a life of value, joy, and true power. Life without service is hollow and has no real power."

I was also eager to know Julia's personal life, particularly whether she had adopted children. "I am joyfully single," she clarified. "I love my independence and being my own woman. I am not averse to being in a relationship, but I haven't met anyone yet who is inspiring enough to make me want to be in one. I still plan to adopt, but it won't be until a few years from now."

80

I believe you can have both—Prince Charming and an adventurous life.

Warrior of the Sea
✦ ✦ ✦

LISA DISTEFANO

At first, the news came from my friends in Indian country. Since 1992, the year I moved from Europe to Los Angeles, I had been getting direct information about Native issues from many reservations across the United States. I have always been interested in Native American culture, and I made a point of reporting what was going on in Indian territory for the Italian press once I moved to the United States. Although unreported in national newspapers, talks about the Makah tribe's return to whale hunting had started as early as 1995. That year, the gray whale population reached twenty thousand again, a number substantial enough to cast them off the list of endangered species. Neah Bay, a small village on the Olympic Peninsula in Washington State where Makahs live, was making way for the comeback of the traditional whale hunt.

81

Makahs were fierce whale hunters until 1930, when concerns of extinction sparked strict environmental regulations. Like the buffalo by the Plains Indians, whale was hunted by the Makahs for survival: The meat fed the people, and the fat kept them warm and their lanterns lit during long winter nights.

Many would have died of hunger and cold without the whales' sacrifice. The tribe hunted the whale the traditional way, chasing her through bay waters, paddling fiercely by canoe, wearing nothing but loincloths, almost as naked as the whale, man and great beast braving the elements in a fight for survival.

They killed the gray whales one at a time with a precise harpoon shot to the head. Hit or miss, it was a loyal chase. It was a ritual hunt whose every aspect was marked with spiritual power, from the canoe to the storage boxes for knives and harpoon heads. Makahs were respectful of the animal that gave up her own life so the people could keep theirs. After they harpooned her, they dragged her to shore, where they prepared a big feast to honor her spirit and give thanks for her sacrifice.

At the approach of the second millennium, Makahs were no longer dependent on the whale for their survival. Long before 1997, when the tribe finally got the green light from the International Whaling Commission to hunt and kill up to five whales each year, I was bracing myself for the inevitable controversy.

It is true that Makahs are the only Native Americans who have a treaty, signed in 1855, that specifically allows whale hunting. Yet renewing such a tradition at this time in history appears unnecessary and cruel. I have mixed feelings myself. Although I usually sympathize with indigenous people's rights to defend their own, and also endangered, cultural traditions,

LISA DISTEFANO

my participation in Indian ceremonies has taught me that it is not right to sacrifice an animal's life unless preserving your own life depends on it.

I was not surprised, therefore, to hear that some environmentalist groups were going to stand against the Makah hunt. Some of this opposition would follow the regular path of petitions and appeals in the quiet halls of legislative agencies, but there were also rumors of different kinds of subversive actions, which would allegedly be carried out by two vessels of the Sea Shepherd Conservation Society, already anchored in Neah Bay.

I already knew about Sea Shepherd and its founder, Captain Paul Watson, cofounder of Greenpeace. Watson left the organization in 1977, disgusted with its newfound political agenda that, in his opinion, involved trying to turn what had once been an ecoactivist group into a soulless, bureaucratic corporation.

Watson organized Sea Shepherd just months after leaving Greenpeace, and with a very different policy in mind. Captain Watson and Sea Shepard's members refused to sit by a fax machine and wait for government answers to their petitions for the survival rights of dolphins, whales, and other sea mammals being barraged and often brutally killed in Japanese waters or on Canadian shores.

As a guardian of sea life, Sea Shepherd hunts the hunters whose policies contradict everything the organization stands for; members go into all-out battle on the hunters' turf. In true pirate fashion, Sea Shepherd advises the whalers to get out of the way, and when they don't, Sea Shepherd rams the hunting vessels with its own ships. This warrior strategy earned Sea Shepherd a controversial reputation and landed its founder in jail in Canada. Some consider Captain Watson and his followers heroes. Others consider them as extreme as ecoterrorists.

When I was first looking into Sea Shepherd in October

1998, I didn't know that one of the "pirates" leading the organization in Neah Bay was a woman. I found out about her in the *Seattle Post-Intelligencer*. According to the report, Lisa Distefano was a thirty-five-year-old of Italian origin, the wife of Captain Watson, the captain of the second vessel anchored in the Olympic Peninsula bay, and the international director of Sea Shepherd. It was a lucky coincidence, since I was an international journalist wanting to cover the story.

Lisa was very warm and welcoming when I first called her from Los Angeles. I explained that I wanted to understand both Sea Shepherd and the Makahs' points of view, since I'd be covering the story for an Italian news magazine. I wanted to meet Lisa and her husband, and I'd also be arranging a meeting with the chairman of the Makah tribe, Keith Johnson, and the members of the "warrior party" who would board the cedar dugout canoe as soon as the first whale was spotted. Lisa was self-assured enough to appreciate my attempt to be objective.

Not long after my first conversation with Lisa, I boarded a flight to Seattle and drove the rest of the way to Neah Bay, just a few hours away. Once I arrived, I walked up and down the pier, surrounded by a thick fog, waiting for the inflatable Zodiac Lisa had arranged to pick me up. She had invited me to meet with her on her vessel, since they were on alert watch and a captain can never abandon her crew during risky moments.

I accepted gladly. I was as interested in Lisa herself as I was in the story of the Makah hunt; my mind was churning with questions about her choice to live as a "pirate." The more I communicated with Lisa and researched her involvement in the cause she sought so valiantly to advance, the more she appealed to me for her uncommon and contagious enthusiasm, bravery, and fearless determination. So I was very pleased about her invitation to have me aboard her vessel, as

84

I'd get a glimpse of her daily life—her duties and pleasures, her victories and losses. *All part of a warrior's life,* I thought as I paced.

The nineteen-foot inflatable Zodiac stops a few feet from the edge of the platform where I've been waiting. Sea Shepherd vessels aren't allowed inside the breaker wall, and even their smaller watercrafts are not permitted to dock on reserve in Neah Bay. "To avoid incidents with the Indians," says the police ordinance. One of the two young guys aboard launches me a rope, signaling to me to tie it around the tall totem pole topped by an eagle head, meticulously carved and painted red, black, and white.

The totem pole sits at the end of the pier; the eagle's eyes look at some distant point in the ocean. I'd seen a similar work of native art in front of the local museum the night before, when I went, by invitation of the Makah council, to attend a spiritual propitiatory ceremony with traditional storytelling and singing. The whales' singing is believed to be the voices of the ancestors, teaching songs that the people believe are important to learn to honor the whales so they will "accept" the tribes' hunting them.

I was captivated by the impressive murals painted on the interior walls of the museums, and by the sculptures depicting hunts of long ago. I was struck by the integral importance of the whale in the Makah culture.

The Makah have become loggers in modern times. Yet they remain highly skilled artisans who can give bare wood amazing life and energy, imbuing it with history and cultural significance.

On the Zodiac, we wait. "Two new members of the crew are supposed to be arriving from Germany," the driver tells me.

Sea Shepherd volunteers come from all over the world

85

and take their places aboard the vessels for shifts of a month or two. They are not paid, and their travel expenses are not refunded. The volunteers are eager to do their part and happy to contribute to something considered heroic by its followers. Were they to volunteer with Greenpeace, it would take them up to three years of copying and filing petitions before they would even see, much less board, a ship at dock.

As soon as Anne and Hans arrive, the three of us take our places on the bench in front of the two drivers who have been waiting with me. The Zodiac zips out to sea at full speed. Rain pours suddenly from the thick clouds lying low against the otherwise clear waters of Puget Sound.

It is a fast, wet, bumpy run, as the Zodiac smacks loudly against the waves and the drivers hurry to escape the wet coldness. But I am happy to be here, breathing this chilly air, and excited to meet a real-life pirate woman.

The *Sea Shepherd III,* as Lisa's ship is named, appears suddenly out of the gray quilt of fog, and it is quite a sight. Beautiful paintings of waves, dolphins, and whales grace its head and flanks. Shades of blue, white, gray, and turquoise alternate to create depth and relevance that recall brilliant summers on the now-murky waters.

The *Sea Shepherd III* is as powerful as it is handsome. At 180 feet in length and 657 tons, and with a one-inch-thick, riveted, welded steel hull, she was built in 1956 as a Norwegian fisheries research and enforcement ship. She is a long-range, ice-class, heavy-duty vessel built to withstand the violent pounding of the storm-haunted North Sea. Sea Shepherd purchased her in 1996 in Edinburgh, Scotland.

I spot Lisa standing on the forecastle dock, dressed entirely in black with long, wavy hair that almost matches her sable outfit. She's looking at the horizon through binoculars, which I watch her pass to one of her crew members as she hears the Zodiac approach.

LISA DISTEFANO

"Welcome aboard!" Lisa offers her sturdy hand as if it's a hook that we should grab onto for additional support as we maneuver up a rope ladder, climbing one unbalanced rung at a time. She leads the newly arrived German crew members to their deckhouses, postponing meeting them until a later time. She takes me to the charthouse and shows me, on the map, the route the gray whales will follow. Every fall, they migrate south from the icy waters of the Aleutian Islands, heading to Baja California and on to the warmer Gulf of Mexico, where they bear their offspring. The following spring, they return with their calves to their Arctic feeding grounds.

"We are on 24/7 alert," Lisa explains while she leads me to the much more comfortable stateroom, where only the captain has the privilege to sleep and spend time away from the crew when she needs to relax and think. She leads me to a leather couch, where we sit and Lisa continues her briefing.

"The alarm started on October first, the day the marine biologists have established as the official beginning of the migratory season. This natural cycle could turn into a bloody horror show this year in Neah Bay, thanks to the federal authorization granted to Makahs. It wouldn't be any different from the carnage of harp and hood seals that the Canadian government allows in Newfoundland. I was hoping that America might do better, but evidently, I was wrong."

The captain has bright, almost transparent emerald eyes and pinkish cheekbones that blush easily in the salty breeze. She wears a black t-shirt that proudly announces, in bold block letters across the back, a complete list of the ships rammed by Sea Shepherd vessels all over the world. Lisa's most recent mission was in Newfoundland the previous spring.

"Each year, the Canadian government authorizes the slaughtering of more than three hundred thousand seals, including babies. They're harmless and peaceful and completely helpless, but they get brutally killed by money-hungry hunters who batter them on the beach with bats and sticks. I will never forget the blood smell and the red mantle spreading across the white ice bank. It was horrific!"

A picture on the wall shows Lisa with her arms wrapped around a fluffy, furry baby harp seal. "Her mom had just been killed, and the baby was desperate. We rescued her and others on our boat, and we took them away from that massacre scene," Lisa recounts in a way that makes me think about all the ways sea mammals must be very similar to us emotionally.

I look at her, trying to imagine whether she was able to comfort and relieve those puppies with her maternal ways, and I see a nurturing ocean crusader, an adoptive "mama" for all marine creatures threatened by human ignorance and greed.

Lisa continues passionately, "The pelts are sold mainly in Denmark and Eastern Europe, and the young seals' penises are worth $60 each in the Asian markets. They are the main ingredients used in remedies said to fight impotence. Hunting baby seals is a barbaric atrocity, and the reason behind it is purely financial. In the Makah case, the reasons appear to be cultural. But those who know international laws regulating fishing and hunting rights in United States waters suspect that the interests of foreign countries like Japan and Norway are hiding behind the Makahs' motives. These countries are hoping to break the protection barrier using the advocated Natives' rights as a spearhead."

Lisa Distefano speaks with the competence of a political leader and the incendiary conviction of a revolutionary. She laughs when I mention that Makahs have listed "health reasons," among others, such as cultural motives like reviving their pride, as grounds for reinstituting their hunting tradition. Makahs believe reintroducing sea mammal meat into

88

their diet is necessary to stave off modern health epidemics like diabetes and obesity.

"There is no scientific evidence to argue that sea mammal meat provides better nourishment than other types of seafood. The gray whale is actually valued more for her fat than for her meat. The meat is tough. It's utilized mainly as an ingredient for commercial dog food. I bet not one of the Makahs asserting their right to better health from seal mammal meat would enjoy the taste. Only a few of the elders can even remember what it tastes like, and they've all said beef's a lot better. Juvenile diabetes and obesity are spread by industrial processed foods, and chips and sodas are Native kids' snacks of choice, just as they are for Caucasian, Latino, and African American kids, when they're plopped down in front of the television. I'm more open to discussing the whale's value in Makah culture.

"In fact," Lisa goes on, "nobody wants to admit it, but the world didn't stop in 1920. Today there are other ways to honor this connection to the whales than by killing them. We've tried to suggest to the tribe that a whale-watching business led by Makahs and enriched by their storytelling could attract tourism to Neah Bay and thereby help their tribal economy."

To substantiate her account, Lisa procures papers and pictures out of a file cabinet and fans them out in front of me. "These people are Stephen and Wendy Dutton, both experienced boat captains and leaders of an animalist group in Monterey. They're working on a documentary for *National Geographic* about the gray whales' migratory journey. We arranged for them to meet Makahs. They volunteered their help to get the tribe started with the whale-watching project. They would have supplied the managing force and even funding, but the tribe refused their offer. Why? Wouldn't that have been a great cultural and financial opportunity that would have avoided spilling innocent blood?"

The alarming sound of a siren interrupts Lisa's explanation. The radar has intercepted a whale vibration about thirty miles east of the *Sea Shepherd III*. Lisa jumps from the couch and storms out the door, shouting for everybody to get ready.

Doors slam and the aisles swarm with swift crew members running and bumping into each other, anxious to reach their assigned emergency positions. I run too, trying to keep up with Lisa, determined not to miss one moment of what is about to happen.

On the deck, Lisa and three others rush down the same rope ladder I barely managed to climb aboard upon. The rain has stopped, and seagulls now patrol the sky. I look over the parapet and spot a small submarine flanking the ship. Painted black and white, it looks like a killer whale, the number one predator of other whales.

"It even sounds like a killer whale," says the second officer, who approaches me after Lisa descends. He's in command anytime Lisa leaves the ship. "We bought it from the Norwegian Navy and equipped it with ultrasounds recorded in the North Sea. Hopefully, the migrating whale will flee as soon as she hears the sound. Hopefully, she'll escape before Makah sentinels spot her and trigger the start signal to the canoe crew."

The canoe Makahs use for the whale hunt is traditionally made from a hollowed-out cedar trunk. Before this moment, the canoe crew has only appeared once before to show off their craftsmanship to a host of reporters. After that, the canoe was returned to a secret place and hasn't been spotted since.

The captain and the other seven members of the warrior party have been elected by the Makah general council and represent all the family clans.

Staying true to tradition, the crew has undergone many purification rituals. Part of the ritual involves the captain's wife's lying still on the floor, in silence and prayer, until the hunt is over, exactly as it was done a century ago.

90

Lisa looks through binoculars, trying to spot the Sirenian *with her husband aboard.*

The killing method has changed, however. The Makah plan to obey the International Whaling Commission's request to spare the dying whale unnecessary suffering by using both a harpoon and a rifle. The harpooner will launch a stainless steel handheld harpoon, mounted on a seven-foot-long wooden shaft and connected to both buoys and the canoe by ropes. The rifleman will fire a specially designed .50 caliber rifle right when or right after the harpoon is thrown. The Coast Guard will make sure other boats stay at least five hundred feet away from the canoe.

As the *Sea Shepherd III* mans the deck, it becomes increasingly clear that the Makah canoe is not headed out to sea. As it turns out, the whale intercepted by the radar was one individual member of a small orca population residing in the Strait of Juan de Fuca.

Warrior of the Sea

"Actually," Lisa tells me when she returns from the "scare-away-blown-away" mission, "we realized she wasn't a gray whale as soon as we spotted her spouting and rolling in the surf. Gray whales are strong bodied and lack a dorsal fin. They have a low hump in its place and are mottled with dark to light gray spots and encrusted with barnacles. The spout is heart shaped when viewed from behind. A few gray whales make their home in Puget Sound, but Makahs are only allowed to hunt migratory gray whales."

Some hunting advocates say gray whales now outnumber the available food sources. They eat about 250,000 pounds of worms and crustaceans collected along the ocean floor during a 130- to 140-day feeding period, a daily average of about 1,850 pounds per whale. There have been huge changes in the ecosystem of the Bering Sea in the past several years, and the large number of grays that have washed up on the beaches of Mexico and California may indicate a dwindling food supply.

When I bring this up to Lisa, she opines quickly and sharply, "Yeah, right! There are also too many children for the available food in Africa, but we don't allow cannibals to exterminate them just to keep a balance."

Lisa is bright, well read, and well aware of how delicate this matter is. "Look," she admits, "I understand that governmental whale-hunting permission for Makahs is small compensation compared to all the abuses they've had to suffer in the past. Sea Shepherd has always had a good relationship with indigenous peoples; we've even fought battles together. This time we're on opposite sides. That's happening, in my opinion, because these Indians have aligned themselves with the same point of view other men have—men from very different backgrounds, perhaps—and have worked with those men to

LISA DISTEFANO

kill too many whales, endangering their existence while transforming the ocean into a sewer.

"No other animal on this planet is stupid enough to endanger its own water sources, not even rodents. Some Makah elders understand this. A few of them, like Alberta Thompson, don't want any more whales to be killed and have spoken out against it in their council. But the majority of the tribe is showing the same ignorance and disregard for the future of our next generations as the white man has shown before them. In this case, I'm not afraid to stand against them."

Political correctness is not of much concern when you're a pirate defending whales. Lisa's duties also include taking care of the humans on her ship. Today she has promised pizza and artichoke-and-cheese pie to her crew. Fresh aboard from the airport, Anne's first shift as the new cook will be postponed a day so she can settle in.

"I was born in North Carolina," says Lisa as she leads me downstairs, bursting with seemingly nonstop energy, "but my father is Italian, from Sicily. I learned to cook from his mom, so I cook like a woman from the South of Italy: fresh ingredients, strong taste, and big portions!"

A standing ovation from the crew greets her in the kitchen, confirming the power of her constant charisma. Her crew treats her like the boss, but also like a teammate, with both respect and camaraderie. On a blackboard above the stove, today's menu is spelled out: OLD TIMER SICILIAN PIZZA AND CRUELTY-FREE POT PIE. "I'm good with slogans, too," Lisa, who spent six years working in advertising before she found her most recent calling, jokes.

After lunch we go back to her quarters, where she volunteers the story of her abrupt awakening. "It was in 1992. I had been a Sea Shepherd supporter since the beginning, even though I was only fifteen when it was founded. I had pictures of Paul Watson all over my room. He was my hero!"

93

. Different emotions roar in the sea of Lisa's eyes as she describes the pivotal event that inspired her career change. "One day, when I had already been working in advertising in Los Angeles for several years, I stayed late at work. It was dark when I walked to the parking lot. A man I'd never met before came toward me, asking for directions. Just a moment before he reached me, I noticed that he was wearing surgical gloves. I tried to run for my car as fast as I could. I made it, but he stopped me from slamming the door shut in his face by wedging his gun in the door just as I was closing it. He raped me right there in my own car. When he was finished, he told me to remain still and silent for an hour. He told me if I disobeyed, he would know and come back and kill me."

Lisa is now speaking slowly, without the signature smile that usually lights up her face and gives her eyes extra shine. She is overshadowed by the memory of the traumatic experience that propelled her toward a wholly different future. "I was petrified. I remained there for what felt like a never-ending amount of time, watching the memories of my life play out, as if on an imaginary screen. All of a sudden, I felt the urgency of changing my life completely. It was time to give up the high-paying corporate job that wasn't making me happy. I was thirty, and I wasn't fulfilling any of the expectations I had once had for myself. It was high time to live by my own values and work to make a difference."

Lisa breaks free from the soft-spoken, self-hypnotizing tone she has sunk into while returning to that moment, and once again she becomes the enthusiastic, inspirational, effervescent speaker who draws people to her. "The day after the attack, I quit my job. I took a big leap of faith and became a full-time volunteer for Sea Shepherd. I've always loved animals of all kinds, but I never fully believed that one individual without political connections could do much for them. Paul's actions and successes have shown me differently. Sea Shepherd has also taught me that it's better to focus your efforts in one direction. I love all animals, but I've always felt most drawn to marine creatures. Sea Shepherd has taught me to embrace that passion."

Lisa laughs, remembering how she had to give up shopping for new clothes every time a store had a big sale. "Of course, I had to learn frugality. It wasn't until 1996 that I obtained one of the very few paid positions in the organization. The good thing was that, once away from the pressure of looking like a Los Angeles career girl, I stopped starving myself and let my size be whatever it was meant to be. Shopping for fancy clothes was no longer as appealing to me as a good, hearty meal. Obviously, I weighed more than I had in my younger modeling years. But I lost the insecurity and the conviction that told me I had to be slim to find love. Love—even attraction—has nothing to do with weight and size. This is just one of the many lessons I've learned from meeting Paul."

I ask Lisa to tell me more about her husband. Her eyes brighten every time she mentions his name. "I'm not kidding when I say he was my hero. The other girls in my college dorm used to tease me, calling him my Prince Charming. Truth is, he was. And in the end I married him, just like in a fairytale."

It just so happens that I will have the privilege of meeting her Prince Charming, as he is expected to arrive that day. Lisa gets excited, much like a schoolgirl half her age would, about the arrival of Paul Watson's ship, the *Sirenian.*

Within an hour, she gets a call by radio. "He's nearly here. Come meet him! You'll see for yourself!" The *Sirenian* seems to be bearing down on us fast, with a black skull-and-crossbones flag billowing in the wind. It is a former United States Coast Guard patrol boat, built in 1955. It has powerful new engines that were installed in 1979 and—I am told—can catch just about any vessel that travels by water. The *Sirenian*'s captain, Lisa's pirate love, is a big man with a full head of silver hair,

95

rough hands, and a kid's smile. He's quite a lot older than Lisa, but he's not paternalistic. He seems as excited as Lisa, warmly embracing her when they see each other.

He comes aboard with only one other man, whose sole focus is getting his hands on the pizza leftovers he's been anticipating all day. I shake hands with Captain Paul Watson and then leave the two of them alone while I mingle with the rest of the crew. We gather in the kitchen, where everyone tells me about their personal reasons for joining Sea Shepherd.

Anne, the new German chef, has already taken her place in the kitchen, despite assurances that she doesn't have to start until the following day. She tells me she was a violinist before selling her apartment in Hamburg to join Sea Shepherd. Simon was a commercial fisherman in Scotland until his early forties. Tired of killing fish, he decided to give back to the ocean and became the chief engineer aboard the *Sea Shepherd III*.

Forty-five minutes go by in a flash. Captain Watson has to leave, boarding the *Sirenian* without satisfying his pizza craving. He heads back to his own surveillance post, and Lisa rejoins me in the kitchen, where I ask her to tell me more about her husband. "Paul was my destiny. Yet our life is not the same as that of most married couples, of course. When we're at sea on a mission, we see each other for a handful of minutes each day, just like today, and then he remains in my sight thanks only to binoculars. But I don't feel abandoned or alone. Togetherness goes beyond the barriers of time and space. Sometimes we stay out at sea for months, never going back to our apartment on land. We talk through crackling radio lines, since cellular phones are out of range this far out at sea.

"Sometimes the separation we have to endure is very hard, though, like it was two years ago, when Paul had been arrested in Canada and I could only see him through glass in a prison there, as if he were a fish in an aquarium. Nevertheless, neither Paul nor I would trade our adventures for a quieter, more ordinary life. Our future, instead of children and a little white house in the suburbs, convertibles, and minivans, will instead be full of baby seals, battleships, the ice floes of Labrador, and the aurora borealis of Alaska. It is an untamed and insecure future. It's as wild as the life we're trying to protect for whales and other ocean creatures. But I can finally say that I'm living my dream."

EPILOGUE

Makahs didn't kill any whales in 1998, and after two months, Sea Shepherd's vessels left Neah Bay. They came back in 1999, but they were unable to prevent Makahs from harpooning and finishing off a two-year-old defenseless whale, which Makah elder Alberta Thompson named Yabis, the Makah word for "beloved."

On December 20, 2002, the U.S. Ninth Circuit Court of Appeals put a stop to the Makahs' rights, asserting that whale hunting violates the Marine Mammal Protection Act. The Court also ruled that a treaty-based activity must conform to both the National Environmental Policy Act and the Marine Mammal Protection Act.

The *Sea Shepherd III* was first renamed *Ocean Warrior* in 1999, and then again *Farley Mowat* in 2002 following the appointment of the new Sea Shepherd international chair, who took Lisa's place. The *Sea Shepherd* flagship was reregistered in Canada and officially began its career in the waters off Costa Rica as a defender of marine wildlife.

The *Sirenian* was sabotaged in the fall of 1999 while docked in Seattle during a standoff with whale-hunt advocates. Recovered and fully overhauled, the *Sirenian* left Seattle at the end of November 2000 to assume guard duty in

Galapagos National Park, where park rangers on twenty-four-hour antipoaching patrol operate it today.

Lisa Distefano and Captain Paul Watson eventually separated and divorced. Captain Watson remarried and is still working as the chief commander of the Sea Shepherd Conservation Society (SSCS) voyages.

But Lisa Distefano vanished, as did many pirate queens before her. She retired from the board of SSCS and from the public scene. Since then, nobody knows her whereabouts.

98

I discovered that when a person finds her own art, she hardly wastes time and energy complaining or regretting once she gets old.

Unlikely Scientist

POLLY MATZINGER

She dropped out of college for fear that whatever career she chose that required a graduate degree would be too darn boring. She didn't get married because she couldn't find a man who held her interest after a few months. She decided she wanted to become a composer and learned to write music. But she found the music she wrote was boring—even to her. She was in love with animals, so she thought why not become a veterinarian? But the schools she applied to rejected her because she had once been a Playboy Bunny.

Meet Polly Matzinger, world-renowned immunologist, former dog trainer, jazz musician, and cocktail waitress. I track her down in her laboratory at the National Institutes of Health in Bethesda, Maryland, where she has been working for the past fifteen years.

99

I saw Polly for the first time on TV in 1998. I was watching the BBC channel and was mesmerized by a documentary called *Turned on by Danger,* produced by Horizon Films and featuring Dr. Polly Matzinger: "Dr. Polly Matzinger is a sheepdog trainer, former Playboy Bunny, and one of the world's foremost immunologists," a voice announced. "Four Years ago she had a blinding moment of insight that led to a most extraordinary idea."

The documentary went on to explain that for half a century, doctors have been taught that the body's immune system attacks anything that's foreign. But Dr. Matzinger is the main proponent of a radical theory called the "Danger Model" that begs to differ: The idea that the immune system operates by attacking all foreign bodies does not explain how we tolerate the millions of "good" bacteria that colonize our digestive tracts, nor does it explain why pregnant women do not reject their babies, which would presumably be recognized by the body as foreign. In Dr. Matzinger's opinion, the body attacks anything that attacks it. "Our immune system responds not to foreignness, but to danger."

The documentary also explained that Dr. Matzinger's theory had led to a revolution in transplant surgery, suggesting ways for conducting transplants that would minimize the risk that the body would reject necessary immunosuppressive drugs. Horizon had filmed something that had never been done before: a mouse receiving a rat's heart in transplant surgery. Such a transplant is considered so foreign that the physicians assumed the heart would be immediately rejected. Yet this mouse, on no drugs and with a completely normal immune system, accepted the rat's heart.

Dr. Matzinger's Danger Model also inspired novel cancer therapies. A patient at one of London's leading teaching hospitals had been injected with bacteria in the hope that the injection would trigger a danger response, arousing his immune system to attack his cancer. And it seemed to be responding.

The documentary focused on the curious path that had led Dr. Matzinger to become who she is today, an esteemed but unlikely scientist. As Dr. Matzinger spoke about her life, she appeared to be a concentrated mix of passion, intelligence, and joy. She appreciated everything and everyone who had blessed her life. Her young, enchanting voice was at once authoritative and musical. Her stream of words and laughter was like pure wine, red and sparkling, pouring from a just-uncorked bottle.

A few years later, when I reach her to confirm that we will meet in person again, she welcomes my call with that same refreshing tone. Over the years we have had a few telephone conversations, and once I decide to include her as one of the women to be profiled in my book, she happily obliges my request to talk again. She suggests that I call her at 5:30 AM, apparently the only hour she can find some quiet time. I'm a night owl, so even though it's only 2:30 AM in Los Angeles, and I woke up at 7:30 the morning before, I'm game. We end up talking at length, sharing more and more about our lives, passions, and mutual love of dogs.

On her side of the country, in her house in Bethesda, "even the dogs are still asleep, so I can steal that time just for myself," she says in a hushed tone.

She tells me to bear with her while she puts on some coffee to fire up her neurons, and then she's all mine, ready to recount her story.

"I was living in Davis, California, in 1973. UC Davis is a very good university, particularly for science and technology.

101

But I wasn't interested. At age twenty-six, I had given up on college. I had decided that corporate America was not for me, so I was making a living working different jobs. I was a dog trainer by day and a cocktail waitress by night. At the end of the day, with tips included, my income rivaled that of a computer technician. And I was happy.

"I've always tried to do whatever I do the best way I can. I'm a good waitress. I'm a great dog trainer, too. In fact," her voice loudens with pride, "just yesterday I was informed that two of my dogs and I have been chosen to be part of the American team at the next World Sheepdog Trial. I'm so excited! It's like the Olympics for dog trainers. It's held every three years. This year it's in Ireland, and for the first time the United States has been invited to participate. It's not totally for sure, because so far there are thirty dogs on the American team and mine hold twenty-ninth and thirtieth place, but things could change and we could still get eliminated."

"Let's hope not," I say, and I mean it. I can tell by the enthusiasm in her voice how much she wants to participate. (Months later I will find out through a follow-up call that her dogs have placed and that she's officially part of the team.) I steer Polly back to her days in Davis.

"Right. Let's get back. The dogs will come with us anyhow because they're part of the story. If it weren't for them, I wouldn't be sitting here now."

Polly isn't exaggerating. I remember from a previous conversation that her first inkling of a theory that would completely overhaul the way science looked at the immune system came from her observations of sheep. "I've trained sheepdogs since I was eleven years old. I've spent mornings hiking with them and teaching them tricks. When I was living in Davis, I was observing sheep one day with my dogs. I noticed a flicker in the grass that signaled imminent danger. A coyote was probably nearby, and the sheep started to bleat, alarmed. My two sheepdogs jumped up, charging toward the danger to protect the flock.

"I considered the idea that our immune system probably works the same way, and that its responses are probably triggered by a danger signal. Everything I had ever read said the contrary, claiming that the immune system reacts when invaded by so-called external agents. But if that's the case, then why don't the immune systems of pregnant women react to the sudden presence of an embryo in the womb? Why doesn't the immune system destroy the fetus? I started to wonder if maybe immune responses weren't triggered only by external agents. It seemed to me that danger signals could be sent by perfectly healthy cells that were already residing in the body.

"Much later, in 1994, I wrote my theory in scientific terms, stating that a specific immune response develops as a result of danger detection, rather than discrimination between self and non-self antigens. What that means is that the immune system detects and then responds to anything dangerous but not to everything foreign. It's as if the body were a community that welcomes visitors with no prejudice but is ready to call the cops when somebody starts breaking the windows."

One day in Davis, Polly happened to eavesdrop on a conversation between two regular customers at the bar where she was working at the time. They were professors of science at UC Davis, discussing the mysteries of the immune system. Polly knew them well enough to feel comfortable telling them her ideas about the topic.

Both scientists thought her observation was original and stimulating. They suddenly looked with different eyes at the pretty girl in a miniskirt and high heels who had been serving them drinks for months. One of the two, a popular professor in his fifties whom his students called Swampy, saw something in Polly worth cultivating.

"Swampy started to bring in articles from scientific magazines and academic journals. He was trying to show me that science is not boring, and that it was worth some sacrifice, despite my decision to never set foot in college again. He was also very warm and encouraging. He gave me a lot of positive reinforcement. But he was not the primary reason I decided to go back to school. Instead it came about as a result of what I had witnessed in the field. I gathered that science allows a person a certain freedom of expression, even if her opinion differs from the main view. If some theory doesn't make sense to you, you can say that without being fired immediately. I thought that was a perfect match for somebody like me who's opinionated and straightforward to begin with."

It wasn't until later on in her career that Polly would find out that freedom of expression actually is limited, even in science. "I think this happens because we have nonscientists governing the lives of scientists. At a very high level, politics also rules science. I'll give you an example: There's a young researcher at the National Institutes of Health who's found evidence of a gene for homosexuality. He hasn't been drummed out of science, but he's having extreme difficulties getting scientists to believe him.

"And the funny thing is, everybody knows there's a gene for homosexuality in fruit flies. Yet the idea that there could be a gene influencing human sexual orientation falls into that gray area where there's no freedom to conduct the study the way you really want to, or to find the answers that are there. Political people don't like answers that counter their belief systems."

104

Polly is fascinated by the relationship between genetics and behavior, and she's not afraid to voice things that might be controversial; "I have a brain and a mind; I'm a scientist with opinions," she notes.

Her own family history has also contributed to her fascination with genetic science. She's learned about some of the genetic experiments performed in concentration camps during World War II and has long been intrigued by the eugenics debate that emerged from Hitler's policies.

"My father is Dutch. He was in the resistance in Holland during the war. He got caught and spent four years in Dachau. At the end of the war, he was the only survivor of the group of prisoners he was in, and he decided to go to France while he decided what to do next. He met my mother there, but he told her immediately that he didn't want to live in Europe anymore. He was afraid of Germany and afraid of Russia. I don't blame him."

Polly's mother's story is equally remarkable: She was a nun in a French convent, but "after five years of novitiate and just before marrying God, she started to have some doubts. She asked for a year's extension, and then in the end, she quit.

"Out of the convent, she decided that if she was ever going to have a normal life, she needed to learn what to do about men. So she went on a yearlong culinary tour of Italy, only she wasn't tasting food. She went from one man's bed to the next until she felt like she knew what she wanted. Then she went back to France, remembering a woman she had met at the nunnery who had promised her a job teaching the village children.

"She became a teacher in a village on the French Riviera, an ex-nun who had rekindled her own sensuality. My father was a survivor of a Nazi prisoner camp determined to start on a new, joyful path. He came wandering along the beach in Tamarille where she was camping with two girlfriends.

"They decided to live together within days of meeting each other. I was born in 1947, and one year later, my sister came along. My father was a very talented painter, but his art wasn't enough to support two children. He wrote to his parents in Holland, who had come back from Indonesia when all the foreigners were forced to leave after Sukarno declared independence and started a strong campaign against the presence of foreigners, particularly Dutch.

"My dad called and asked them to help him find a job. But his mother's reaction was anything but positive. She told him she wouldn't help him support his French slut and their two bastard children. So my parents decided to get married, and we went to Holland, where my father became a flight attendant for KLM Airlines."

Touring the world on planes allowed Polly's father to look in earnest for an opportunity to leave Europe, to find a new country where he could start anew with his young family. He had his heart set on America, but after he applied for the family's immigration papers, it took five years for the Matzingers to obtain permission to go there. When they finally arrived in California, Polly was seven years old.

"My dad had chosen Los Angeles, but Watts was the only neighborhood where we could afford to rent a house. Life in such a ghetto community was hard, but it was also an incredible learning experience. Without the years I spent in Watts, I might not be who I am now. I had to struggle to make people forget that I was different. I had to fight prejudice, and I found out at an early age that the best way to do that is to get other people to hear you.

"I didn't try to mask my differences or be somebody I wasn't just to fit in. I wanted to be accepted for who I was. It was worth fighting for. I think it strengthened me."

POLLY MATZINGER

Polly has been strong minded and unconventional all her life, even before she became an unconventional scientist. "It took a really long time to discover what I could be really good at. My family is full of artists. My mom is a great ceramicist, even though she made a living as a teacher. My dad is a painter. My sister is a sculptor, and my brother, who was born in the United States, has become a rock musician.

"I love music, too, especially jazz. So when I first enrolled in college at UC Irvine, I studied music, thinking I wanted to become a composer. But I seemed unable to write anything exciting or really good. I didn't want to be mediocre. And it's hard when you're twenty-two and you realize that you're bad at something you thought was your calling."

I tried to picture Polly at age twenty-two, convinced she couldn't be a musician, and it made me sad. But even though such a situation might be depressing for many young people, that wasn't the case for Polly.

"I just thought, *Oh well, I'll go with plan B,* which was to become a veterinarian, something I'd always been interested in. But when the school I wanted to attend found out that I'd been a Playboy Bunny, they didn't let me in." She doesn't offer more information on that particular phase of her life, and I don't push her for more details.

At that point, unable to find a strong enough incentive to stay in school, Polly dropped out of school. She decided to stick with jobs that were earning her bread and butter. "I wasn't ashamed at all to be a waitress and a dog trainer; I learned from my parents to never judge people by what they do to make a living. My father was a waiter himself occasionally when he couldn't find other jobs, and neither of my parents ever made me feel belittled for what I was doing."

Polly did, however, finally decide she was ready to re-enter the world of college, this time to study science at UC San Diego, and today she is grateful that the University of

California system was flexible enough to welcome her back with no reservations. "It's so refreshing! Education in the United States is very expensive, but people are encouraged to study and go back to school, no matter how old they are. In Europe, on the other hand, although public education is free and state universities are often better than private ones, there is a limited time frame in which to attend them in order to be considered a successful student. So you can't really decide that you made a mistake when you were eighteen years old, and that you want to change your path, or you pay."

After UC San Diego, Polly went on to get her PhD there as well, and did some of her postdoctorate research at the Salk Institute, also in San Diego. After she graduated, she was offered a job in England as a biology researcher in the immunology lab at Cambridge University. "What I appreciated most there was that the intellectual circle was a lot less segregated than in the United States. Scientists are in close contact with economists and artists in Europe, and I think it adds flavor to academic discussions and people's lives in general."

Polly had been married briefly when she was twenty-one, to a drop-dead-gorgeous architect. In Cambridge, she came close to marrying a second time.

"He was a navy pilot who had dropped out of medical school because he thought it was boring. He was rich, too, the kind of guy every mother wants for her daughter. But my mom told me I should live with him first, to do a trial run. We lasted for nine months. When you cry more than you laugh, it's time to leave.

"My mother saved me the second time, too," she laughs. "Same advice. She told me that in order to marry God, who's perfect, you have five years as a novitiate as a trial. In order to marry a human being, who's far from perfect, you'd better have a trial period as well. 'Live with him first,' she advised me again. 'If, after a year, you still want to marry him, then

POLLY MATZINGER

you'll have my blessing.' My mother, the nun. Isn't that amazing? I feel so blessed for having had such amazing parents."

I nod in agreement: Love, just like science, should be fun.

"I have yet to find a man who keeps me amused enough," admits Polly. "I still think it's possible, even if, as the men and I get older, it gets harder. People think elders are wise, but it's only young people who gather wisdom as they age who grow into wise people. Young people who don't have any wisdom grow into horrible old people, very self-righteous and set in their ways. Who wants to have one of those around?"

Of course, living with four dogs provides plenty of companionship. Yet, I ask Polly, does she ever wish she had a significant other?

"There was a time," she says, "when I felt lonely. That happened toward the end of my childbearing years. I was living in Switzerland at that time, a pretty lonely place to live. The hardest times were the holidays. I'd go walking down the streets, and everybody else was walking in pairs, holding hands. I guess I was still thinking that I could start a family with someone. But I wasn't going to settle for someone who wasn't going to be my intellectual match. I need someone who is fun and smart if I'm going to be with that person for the rest of my life."

When she was living in Switzerland, Polly started resenting other things, too. "Every time I was driving my Honda 750, I was stopped by the cops. They weren't used to seeing a woman driving a big motorcycle, so they felt compelled to check me out, just in case something was wrong."

Polly had a hard time with the language too. "I generally have no problem learning languages. In fact, I once delivered a paper at a conference in Japan in Japanese after studying the language for only three months. But the Swiss don't have a native language. There are many different dialects, even though they try to communicate through a common written language, which is German. That might explain why there are not many Swiss poets."

By the end of the eighties, Polly was ready to move to a country where she could speak and work in English again. "It became important to me. I thought Australia was a fascinating possibility, but then I went there to visit and didn't think I would like living there. So in 1989, when I received an offer from the American government to come back and work at the National Institutes of Health (NIH), I was happy. I wasn't prepared, though, to come back to a country that isn't aware of the fact that it lives in a world with many neighbors. You notice these things more when you have been exposed to other cultures. America believes itself to be at the center of the world and to be the ruler of all other nations. But it's not; and if it were, it would imply responsibilities that America is not willing to take."

She leaves this comment hanging in the air. I can tell it affects her deeply, but I don't pursue her political passions, since I'm eager to learn more about her life after returning to the United States.

"But anyhow," she swerves the conversation without prompting, "the story goes that they offered me a position and the opportunity to come back, and I did."

Dr. Matzinger did not start working right away, though. "They hired me and gave me a laboratory and a salary, but I didn't really start working for nine months. I spent all that time studying mathematics. I was interested in chaos theory because I thought that it might have something to say about the immune system. My colleagues at NIH still call my lab the Ghost Lab because it was empty for nine months while I studied math. Finally, for two reasons, I decided I wasn't taking the right approach. First, I saw that it wasn't yet time

110

 Polly (at bottom) draws blood from one of her sheep, aided by two of her assistants.

to try to do the math I was working on to support my theories about the immune system, because there simply weren't enough numbers to work with. To see if a formula works, you have to have some real numbers to test against. The immune system is really a good example of the uncertainty principle: You can't get a number without changing the system. For example, to find out how much antibody a vaccinated individual is making, you have to bleed him. But by bleeding him, you stimulate him to make more antibody. So you won't know how much he's making unless you bleed him again (thereby stimulating him again). Before we can really get at the math of the system, we'll have to devise noninvasive methods to get the numbers.

"Second, I found that I didn't like the process of trying to find formulas that describe the immune system. I would much rather describe it in other ways. In a way, it's a bit like an artist's choosing to depict nature by painting or sculpting or

111

writing poetry or music. Each artist finds the method that calls to them. Mine, in the end, was not the math of chaos theory. I saw that what I really loved was finding the minute details that make the difference between immunity that works and immunity that doesn't. So I went back to the Ghost Lab and started doing experiments."

Everything in Polly's life and work happens because of something. Cause and effect. She has a scientist's philosophical approach to her daily life. "When I finally got back to my lab, I was pleased that my colleagues had nicknamed it the Ghost Lab, because ghosts are spirits, and spirits are a very important thing in science. So I kept the nickname, and it became the lab's official name; it's even published on my papers, even though it can be difficult to convince journals like *Nature* and *Science* to print it. But research is supposed to be fun. We don't do this job because we get paid a lot of money. We do it because it's fun, because it inspires passion, because we are artists." I realize that Polly really has finally found her art in science.

She asks me to tell her a little bit about journalism and whether certain forces keep it from being fun. "Not always," I tell her. "But there are compromises that you need to make as a writer. I, too, do what I do the way I do it because I have fun doing it. And, yes, the money would be better if I compromised more. Yet the freedom of expressing myself the way I want and to communicate with people who might enjoy what I write as seen through my own eyes has no price."

"I guess it's the same with other arts, too," Polly speculates. "My sister and I are having conversations about what's happening to artists with money and art, about how much one influences the other. She's a great sculptor and now, at fifty-six, she's actually quitting. It's so sad. She says no one is buying the art she wants to do. People tell her things like, 'Your art takes me places I don't want to go.' But I say, 'That's powerful!'"

Polly is in the middle of writing her sister a long letter because, she says, "writing is also powerful." She hopes that her sister will think it over and feel encouraged. "In my letter to her, I write about Mozart, because the only artists I know are musicians. I don't really know about visual arts. Mozart didn't write his music to make money. He wrote because he couldn't stop writing. He wrote because it drove him crazy not to.

"I guess part of my sister's problem is that her husband is an accountant. He's a very good husband as it goes, but he has never truly been able to understand that his wife is an artist, and that her brain just works differently. One time her husband actually called me and asked, 'Can you please help me?' And I was like, 'What's your problem?' And the problem was that she was in the sculpting studio until three in the morning and wasn't coming home to cook dinner.

"They've been married since she was eighteen, almost fifty years now, and it's a good marriage in many ways. But now she's having this crisis, and God knows he can't be much help. So I'm trying to find a way to tell her that she can just give away her art for others' enjoyment and for her own happiness, not for money. But I have to be careful because I'm her older sister, even if just by one year, so I don't want to sound like I'm patronizing her."

Polly has a beautiful mind. She's genuinely interested in other people's business. She's generous and caring, encouraging yet aware enough to keep her own strength in check, to avoid becoming bossy. I tell her I'm not surprised she's such a great dog trainer. She laughs.

"Are you suggesting that I'm treating my sister like I treat my dogs? Well, you're actually right. And there is nothing

113

demeaning in that. Dogs are very smart, loyal, and affectionate. They've taught me so much about how to deal with people. I read a lot of books about dog training. Some are absolutely wonderful. One book, *Culture Clash*, by Jean Donaldson, has become a cult book among dog trainers. It's all about how differently dogs and humans behave, and how the two cultures clash. It's a difficult book to read because the author is extremely angry about how people treat dogs. In the first few chapters, you'll find yourself pounding the table and saying, 'I don't like this tone,' but you have to force yourself through that and get to a fictional chapter called "The Gorens," in which she describes these fictional beings who keep humans as pets. I tell you, as good as you are with your dog now, when you're done reading, you'll be different. But the best thing about the book is the tools it provides for bettering your relationships with humans."

Polly is convinced that good dog training is very similar to good academic training.

A lot of Polly's work nowadays is about training young scientists through the NIH. She's the head of the lab and therefore has people training under her constantly.

"You want them to trust you. You want them to bring you their experiments that have failed. You want them to feel comfortable enough to bring you the things they're confused about. What gets in the way is people's pride. They don't want anybody to know about their failures. So you need to provide positive reinforcement so they will bring you their failures, particularly in science. Of course, then you can't slam them to the ground if they've failed.

"I tell my students about this great article, 'To Err Is Human,' by Lewis Thomas, in a series called 'Notes of a Biology Watcher' that he wrote for the *New England Journal of Medicine*. He talks about mistakes in science and how discoveries can only happen by making mistakes.

POLLY MATZINGER

"I also talk to my students about making movies. You start with take one, and if it doesn't work, you go on to take two, and if that doesn't work, either, you're on to take three. Maybe you need 125 takes to find the one that really works for you. So what do you call the ones that didn't work? You called them 'missed takes.' And the difference between a 'missed take' and a mistake is that in a missed take, nobody gets blamed. You just change what needs to be changed and do it again. It's part of the process."

I tell Polly about something Kevin Kelly, author of *The New Economy*, told me some years ago, about how the Internet changed not only the economic structure, but also the values, of business. Failure is no longer considered a stigma or something to hide, at least in more advanced business environments. Failures are part of the experience. Hiring somebody who endured and survived a failure, Kelly explained, can only strengthen the company, since you already know how that person will react to difficulties and have already witnessed firsthand that obstacles will not destroy her.

"There you go!" Polly exclaims. "I wish more of my colleagues were that wise!"

She continues with her previous train of thought. "To communicate with somebody who comes from a different culture, you need to understand their quintessential behavior. You need to make and process observations. When you meet a human, you walk up to him, you look straight into his eyes, and you put out your hand to shake his hand. Try that with a dog.

"Dogs don't do that. Two dogs walking straight at each other signal aggression.

"Sometimes humans cause dogs to become neurotic the same way we are because we are signaling to them—with our

115

human behavior, no matter how inadvertent—that they should somehow make human choices. It forces them into a position of leadership, even though the natural human-dog relationship necessitates that the human being is in charge.

"When dogs are put in a position of leadership in the human-dog dynamic, they get neurotic because there's no way they can do the job.

"Does that ring any bells? It's the same with kids and students. Children and students want and need boundaries. If they're forced to deal with parents and teachers who aren't comfortable with imposing rules and structure, it creates terrible insecurities for the kids. It shifts the power dynamic, sometimes forcing the child or the student to be in charge when they don't have the skills required for the job.

"Dogs have human emotions, but they don't need to have human behaviors. They experience separation anxiety when they are led to believe they should behave like humans. I realized that one of my dogs was experiencing anxiety because some of my behaviors led her to believe that I was her puppy. She was terrified by thunderstorms, and when she would lick me on the nose, I would lick her back, involuntarily instilling in her the sense that I was looking to her for comfort, like a puppy might. I quit doing this in an effort to reassure her that I was in charge, that I was her leader, and that I was there to take care of her.

"And guess what? She's stopped being so shaken when thunderstorms happen. She doesn't hide under a bed anymore. She comes to me to be reassured, and when I pet her she relaxes. She trusts my judgment. She thinks it's okay if I behave as if everything is okay. Dogs can read anxiety as much as they can read calmness, just like children. I think of this when I'm teaching; it's the same type of dynamic I want to foster with my students, and it's the type of relationship any good mentor should strive for."

116

POLLY MATZINGER

Polly's comment jogs my memory, and I ask her about her own mentor's role in her becoming a scientist. I ask her if she and Swampy are still in touch. "This is a very sad part of the story. Actually, it's sad and embarrassing. Swampy is dead now, and I never thanked him for what he did for me. When I graduated, I dedicated my thesis to him. But you know the statement that perfectionism is the enemy of good? Well, I'm a perfectionist. My mother is a perfectionist, and I must have, unfortunately, taken after her.

"So here's what happened. He changed my life, and when I went to graduate school, the first paper I published was a theory paper. I wanted to send it to him, but I thought it wasn't good enough, so I didn't. The next paper I published was my first nature paper. And I thought it was good, but it was a cooperative paper. So I thought, *No, no, I need to send him something when it's all done by myself and perfect.* And then again, when I finished school and wrote my thesis, I dedicated it to him, but I didn't send it to him because that, too, wasn't perfect.

"And then in 1996, two years after I wrote 'The Danger Model,' which I did not send his way, either, and which the BBC came here to film, I finally acknowledged him out loud to the documentarians. I asked them to consider interviewing him. They went, and he was already dead. And I never thanked him. Isn't that awful? Isn't that absolutely disgusting?"

I try to reassure Polly that it's not, that it was a normal response for how she felt at that time. She had wanted to give him her best and felt like nothing was ever good enough.

"Come on!" she nearly yells. "Here is a man who changed my life, and I thought I'd never do anything perfect enough to even acknowledge him? What do you call that? 'Immature' seems to be an understatement. But the good news is, I had another mentor, and he's still alive. His name is Mel Chon. He showed me things from genetics to immunology. He works at

117

the Salk Institute. But when I asked him to take me as a graduate, he said no, it was too dangerous because, he told me, 'if I take you, I know that I could walk out of my lab, look back, and see the whole thing going up in a mushroom cloud.'

"But when I wrote 'The Danger Model,' I sent it to him. For some reason, maybe because he's also a theoretician, I felt it was good enough for him. But he didn't like my theory, and he called me up to tell me so. Still, the man is amazing; in fact, we eventually agreed to disagree and go dancing. We love each other. Arguing with him is great. On the one hand, you feel like you have an equal, and on the other hand, you have a spark, you have a fire, you have a mirror.

"Mel Chon is somebody who never says, 'You're stupid' or, 'You don't study enough.' He argues strictly about science, not about your character. And arguing with him causes you to drag all your hidden assertions out into the light and look at them. We all need this, and I'm so lucky to have a friend and mentor who does that for me."

It's getting really late, or early, for that matter, in Los Angeles. In Bethesda it's nearly time for Polly to go to work. But we keep talking on the phone, and it seems neither of us really wants to be interrupted because, as Polly would say, *we're having fun.*

"My dogs will send you their complaints through their lawyers," Polly jokes. I can imagine her dogs, anxious at the door, waiting for her to finish up and take them out for their hike. I remember that she goes out with them early in the morning, driving through the hills. They park and hike up the trail until they find sheep. She does that at least five times a week, and she calls it her "stolen time," stolen only because the life of a scientist is so all-consuming. For her it's also an escape from the nuisance of the city and the little things we deal with in our daily lives.

POLLY MATZINGER

"Dog training has become my dojo space for meditation. It's also the gym where I warm up the muscles of my mind, readying myself to face what the rest of the day will bring. It's my ongoing philosophical experiment before putting on my scientist's uniform for other experiments. And the meditation of dog training is still all about being a good observer, listener, and leader—just the same qualities you need to succeed at everything else in life."

EPILOGUE

After fifteen years, Polly's work is less about experiments and more about reading and writing papers, discussing and reviewing what others do. She has eight people in her Ghost Lab, and she's the boss. She no longer has a private office with a door, just a desk in the middle of the room.

"It's called management by wandering around," she jokes. "I walk around and look at what my trainees do. I ask questions, comment, discuss their work with them. Once in a while, I still do an experiment, immunizing a sheep or doing some surgery. I take a break and go home for a little while around 2 PM. I don't sleep much at night, but I live only three and a half minutes' biking distance from the lab, so that's my luxury.

"Then, I come back to the lab and I stay late, until ten or eleven or midnight. Unless," she's quick to add, "I have something better to do . . . like go dancing!"

119

I have achieved a leadership position because I am willing to take risks.

Spirited Chief

✦ ✦ ✦

WILMA MANKILLER

Tahlequah sits in the middle of the lusciously green Ozarks foothills, 160 miles south of Tulsa in rural Oklahoma. Here, in one of the most important and populated Indian reservations, are the tribal headquarters of the Cherokee Nation. Since 1987, Cherokees have had a female chief, Wilma Mankiller. It is the first time in their history that such a thing has come to pass. The Cherokee tribe is second in size only to the Dine (Navajo) Nation.

There are historical records of women leading small bands like the Seconnet, who in 1661 elected as their chief a woman named Awashonks, whose fame obscured even that of the male warriors in her family, or the Wampanoag, who voted Wetamoo to be their brave warrior queen from 1662 until her death in 1676, when she was killed by the English. But never before Wilma Mankiller has a woman been the head of such a large number of Indians. There are 140,000 enrolled members of the Cherokee Nation living both on and off the Cherokee reservation in Oklahoma.

Elections will soon be upon the people of the Cherokee Nation, and Wilma Mankiller is determined to submit her candidacy for reelection, hoping to encounter less gender opposition than in 1983, when she ran for deputy chief on the ticket with Chief Ross Swimmer. Although this is a land of rugged cowboys who might prefer to see some of their "good ol' fellas" run for political office, you'd be hard pressed to find many people who find fault with the performance of the Mankiller administration while she has been in office. Even the fact that she's a Democrat and harbors more liberal notions than her mostly Republican-leaning fellow Cherokees doesn't turn heads anymore.

Nor is it as contentious as it once was that she's a "half-breed," the daughter of a full-blood Cherokee father and a Dutch-Irish mother. Wilma Mankiller has proven herself, against many odds, to be an excellent chief since she replaced Ross Swimmer in 1985, when he was called to Washington, D.C., to take on a larger role with the Bureau of Indian Affairs (BIA).

I am going to meet Wilma Mankiller at the suggestion of Dee Brown. He's a writer I have long admired, the author of *Bury My Heart at Wounded Knee*, the classic text on the colonization of Indian tribes in the 1800s, and *The Gentle Tamers*, a book about pioneer women. I wrote him a letter from Italy explaining my intention to track down outstanding women who are trailblazers and asking for ideas about possible candidates. Although many people told me that such a well-known writer was not likely to respond to my request, Brown was kind enough to get back to me with a few names. Mankiller was one of them.

Mankiller is the English translation of the Cherokee word *Asgaya-dihi*. It has survived in Wilma's family as a surname for five generations, although it was originally not a name at all. In the past, it was a rank or title, like "water-goer," used only after one had earned the right to it. There was one *Asgaya-dihi* for each town where the tribal people resided. The *Asgaya-dihi* was in charge of killing enemies after they were taken prisoner, sometimes taking matters into his own hands on the spot for the protection of his town.

Wilma's great-great-grandfather was the *Asgaya-dihi* of Talico in Tennessee, though she says she does not know if her great-great-grandfather actually killed anybody. Talico was part of the original Cherokee land before the shameful forced deportation of Indians, later recorded and widely known as the Trail of Tears, in 1838. The first of those deported numbered around one thousand, but the forced expulsion went on until 1939, and the calculation by today's estimates is in the range of nine to ten thousand Cherokees, four thousand of whom perished in detention camps along the way, and a number of others of whom got lost and never arrived.

"I guess one of the reasons why many Cherokees are Republicans dates back to that deportation," Wilma Mankiller explains to me when I meet with her. "The deportation from our original lands in North Carolina and Tennessee was ordered by President Andrew Jackson. He used the supposed rights granted to him by a treaty signed in 1835 by a handful of misguided Cherokees who didn't have the authority to speak for all Indians. We call Jackson the Big Fat Liar. He was a traitor to the Cherokees, who had been good to him. A chief from those times named Junaluska had even led five hundred of his best warriors into battle against another Indian tribe,

123

the Creeks, in support of the United States Army during the Battle of Horseshoe Bend in Alabama in 1814.

"Junaluska personally saved Jackson's life in that battle. But that did not prevent the American president from ordering the military to escort the Cherokees to their so-called new home. That was the beginning of the Trail of Tears saga, which would ultimately be a twelve-hundred-mile westward trek. Jackson ordered seven thousand soldiers to forcibly escort the Indians to their new home, as if they were prisoners of war, for the entire duration of the operation. Jackson's order was executed by those seven thousand soldiers under General Winfield Scott."

Wilma Mankiller starts the first of several conversations with me in her office at the tribal headquarters in Tahlequah. She sits behind a huge, dark wood desk in an orderly, clean room with law and history books lining multiple shelves behind her. She's wearing a dark skirt suit with a white blouse and a gorgeous pendant hanging from a silver chain. "It's a special pink mother-of-pearl that my people gather on the bottom of Tenkiller Lake," she tells me, noticing the magnetic power the jewel has over me. "They named the pearl after me when I won the elections, and a very talented artist, Knokoutee Scott, from Tulsa, designed this medallion." She is pleased that I like it. I'm very impressed by the way Chief Mankiller combines contemporary business attire and beautiful traditional ornaments. I find her personal style incredibly alluring. And even more than her look, I am compelled by her simple and direct talk. I'm not surprised that she has been able to overcome the prejudice she has encountered against her leadership.

We continue talking about the days when the Cherokees were relocated. Today most Americans agree that the relocation of the Cherokee people is "one of the most infamous chapters in American history." So said John G. Burnett, a soldier fluent in the Indian Cherokee language who was hired as

124

an interpreter by Captain Abraham McClellan, commander of the Second Regiment of Foot and Second Brigade of Infantry trekking through Kentucky, Illinois, Missouri, and Arkansas. It was an exhausting yearlong march to get to northeastern Oklahoma. The army arrived with little less than a third of the Indians the expedition had started with. John Burnett lived in Tennessee and told these stories in his "Eightieth Birthday Story," published in 1890 in the Tennessee local press. The article would be reported on for years to come in many accounts about the Cherokee Trail of Tears.

It was a holocaust, ugly and unwarranted. Of the almost twelve thousand Cherokees deported in 1838 from Tennessee to Oklahoma by foot, wagons, and boats—following the Tennessee River where that was an option—four thousand people died of pneumonia, cold, and other untreated diseases in detention camps. These cold facts have caused historians to refer to the Trail of Tears as the "Cherokee Holocaust" because it led to the extermination of a particular tribal group. Some were forced to walk in shackles. Many became ill or perished because they could not resist the biting cold that arrived and persisted throughout the winter.

When the last group finally arrived in Oklahoma, it was March 1839. In September, the foundation of the Cherokee Nation was established during a four-day meeting in Tahlequah. Chief John Ross and the representatives of the two other main parties, the Old Settlers and the Treaties, remained locked in a room until they came up with the first constitution to be adopted by the unified tribe.

"The Cherokees were considered one of the so-called five civilized tribes, along with the Choctaw, Chickasaw, Creek, and Seminole," Mankiller informs me. "Those were the tribes who had the earliest and most frequent contacts with whites. These were the tribes who most influenced American history and who were influenced most by the newcomers. Cherokees are also said to be the first Indians ever to meet a European, the Spaniard Hernando De Soto, in 1540.

"During colonization, it wasn't rare for Cherokees to take a stand with the Europeans against other tribes. It happened in 1713, when we helped the British push the Tuscarora out of Carolina. It happened again a few years later, when we refused to join the Yamassee conspiracy to kill all whites. We were punished by the Creeks for rejecting the bloody massacre, and in return they ransacked and burned our villages." There is no trace of anger in her, no judgment in her eyes. She repeats all of this information that she carries as a testimony to the harsh treatment her people have suffered. Her disposition evidences her people's natural good temperament and their amazing capacity for forgiveness.

Chief Wilma Mankiller is a charming, elegant woman who embodies the down-to-earth demeanor of a country girl and the straightforwardness and inner fire of an activist. She was born in 1945 and raised in the small, insular Cherokee dominion of Adair County, which claims the highest percentage of Native Americans anywhere in the United States. She's also a true child of the California Sixties. Even now, back in her homeland after enduring her own family's "deportation" to San Francisco in 1956—when she was just eleven years old— she's fond of her memories from California, where she spent twenty-one years of her life.

It was there, Wilma says, that she really bloomed and shaped her invincibility, the strength that supported her through odds and obstacles that would confront her later in life. But it was in Tahlequah, where her roots are, that she forged her temper and built her own value system at a very early age. Cherokee traditional values, like being "of good spirit," have sustained her throughout her life. Wilma makes

126

a conscious effort to blend that ancestral heritage with what she learned from her time in California, and she dances with incredible poise and balance on the border between those two disparate worlds.

Wilma tells her story through a lens of common experiences lived by many other Cherokees, other Indians, and also some non-Indians, which gives her personal story a broader context. She's the spokesperson for the deeply rooted Indian conviction that we're all related, and that the collective must always come before individual needs and pride.

"My family left Mankiller Flats, the land that had been our home for generations, in 1956. Technically, we weren't forced to do anything. Our poverty prompted the move. We were farmers. We had lived off that land since Oklahoma became a state in 1907, when the government forced redistribution of the properties once commonly owned by the tribe, allotting parcels of 160 acres to each family. John Mankiller, my paternal grandfather, was allotted 160 acres in Adair County, on the border of Cherokee County. Right after the war there were several years of drought. Our fields of strawberries and peanuts were not producing enough harvest anymore. There were no available jobs on the reservation to support a family as big as ours.

"Relocation started to look like the only viable option. In 1953, Dwight Eisenhower succeeded President Truman. This also meant a change of command at the BIA. Termination and relocation programs were already being proposed as a way to deal with the 'Indian problem.' Dillon Myer, former director of the Japanese War Relocation Authority, had initiated some of these programs after the Japanese internment following World War II. He accepted Truman's invitation to become the commissioner of the BIA in the early 1950s.

"Myer, a lifelong bureaucrat, had little regard for non-whites and was promptly awarded the position as head of the BIA for having been the diligent keeper of 120,000 men, women, and children of Japanese descent. At least two-thirds of the 'evacuees,' as the government called them, were American born. They were innocent United States citizens, rounded up, removed from their homes all along the West Coast, and placed in tar-paper barracks at the War Relocation Authority (WRA) camps scattered throughout the West. The eleven Japanese American internment camps were built on remote federal land, including two on Indian reservations in Arizona. The camps were surrounded by barbed wire. Military policemen perched in guard towers behind their machine guns were under strict orders to shoot any inmates who tried to escape. These so-called War Relocation Centers were nothing more than concentration camps."

Wilma Mankiller thinks that, in many ways, the assorted Trails of Tears endured by many Indian ancestors served as models for the removal of the Japanese immigrants and Japanese Americans in the 1940s.

"Dillon Myer would have made Andrew Jackson and Indian-fighters Kit Carson and Phil Sheridan very proud. Once at the BIA, he fired most of the officials who really cared about us, those who had tried to defend our land rights. As replacements, he brought aboard his WRA cronies—all of them whites—who knew nothing about Indian affairs or law but were proven 'yes-men.' In Myer's eyes, Indian reservations did not differ much from prison camps. He pointed out that encouragement of subsistence farming, which had been a standard policy during Franklin D. Roosevelt's New Deal years, was no longer a viable solution in the postwar period."

Dillon Myer was convinced that mounting unemployment on reservations was the result of the return of 113,000 Native Americans who had left their land during the war. In his mind, it was useless to try to develop local resources on the reservations, and it would be much better to relocate young

Indians and their families to urban and industrial areas so that they could work—like white people. Giving up government health services, schools, and other privileges would "release" Indians, Wilma summarizes, and "permit them to behave as individuals, mainstreaming and resettling into the general American population."

In 1953, when Eisenhower entered the White House, there was a change of command at the BIA. However, Glenn L. Emmons, a banker and rancher from Gallup, New Mexico, was assigned to the position with the change of administration. Emmons shared the belief that the remedy for Indian unemployment and reservation overpopulation lay in the termination of federal responsibilities for all Indians, and in the relocation of a large number of rural Native Americans to big industrial cities.

Mankiller continues with her story, adding to the history I have already studied. "The BIA used promotional brochures with staged photographs of smiling Indians in 'happy homes' in these big cities. After 1907, when Oklahoma became part of the federal union, our tribal government was abolished, and Cherokees were under the 'protective wing' of the government, as were many other tribes also 'terminated.'

"In 1955, some men from the BIA came to our house. They talked my father into the wonderful opportunities he would find in the big city, into obtaining good educations for us kids and leaving poverty behind once and for all. But I think Dad had mixed feelings at first. As a boy, he had been taken from his home against his will to attend Sequoyah Boarding School, on the same land where the Cherokee reservation is today but in a different county from his home. My dad's generation had to endure being sent to schools where Indian youths were punished for speaking their native language, where they were forced to cut their hair short, as if they were whites."

Sequoyah, whose English name was George Gist, is the

most famous Cherokee, credited with inventing the syllabary of the written Cherokee language. He was born in 1770, a time when Indians thought that mastering the "talking leaves"—as some referred to the white people's ability to communicate with one another by making distinctive marks on paper—was a gift from God. Sequoyah, who was handicapped from a hunting accident and therefore had more time for contemplation and study, spent twelve years working to devise a similar communication system for Cherokees.

Despite criticism and even accusations of practicing witchcraft, in 1821 he was finally ready to demonstrate that the eighty-five characters in his syllabary represented all the combinations of vowel and consonant sounds forming the Cherokee language. "It was amazing," comments Wilma Mankiller. "Sequoyah's discovery resulted in a true cultural revolution for the tribe. Within several months of Sequoyah's unveiling of his invention, a substantial number of people in the Cherokee Nation were reportedly able to read and write in their own language. The Christian missionaries opposed the new syllabary in the beginning but later realized that it could help even their conversion work. In 1827, the council appropriated funding for the establishment of a national newspaper. On February 21, 1828, the inaugural issue of the newspaper *Tsa la gi tsu lehisanunhi,* or *The Cherokee Phoenix*, printed in parallel columns in Cherokee and English, was ready for distribution. It was the first Indian newspaper published in the United States—one more record to be proud of."

As Wilma tells her story, I am captivated by her smooth, eloquent way of speaking. "It didn't come free!" she jokes. "It's the result of whole nights spent reading together with my sister when we were preteens newly arrived in San Francisco. We were so eager to fit in and so worried we would never achieve it. We didn't want to sound and feel like strangers.

"There were low times," she admits. "A lot of them. But I

learned to practice an ancient Cherokee value, being of good spirit: trying to always see the positive in anything. It really makes life easier. It doesn't spare you pain and trials, but it allows you to transform them into learning experiences. It calls for optimism and for humor, two very important tools to shape a good life."

The eleven-year-old Wilma must have needed a lot of humor when she landed in San Francisco in October 1956, at the end of a two-day, two-night train trip with her whole family. What was she thinking? How did she feel? What was her first impression when she descended on the railway tracks into a station where dozens of trains came and went at high speeds, announcing departure and arrival with their sharp whistles? I wish I could slip into the eyes and body of Wilma the little girl as she was then, to see and feel what she was going through.

"It was like landing on the moon," laughs Wilma. "And the culture shock only grew in the following days once we tried to settle—there were ten of us, since my youngest two siblings were not born yet—in our first one-bedroom city apartment in the working-class neighborhood of Potrero Hill. We spent our first two weeks in a sleazy old hotel in the Tenderloin district, where prostitutes swarmed the streets at night. The noises of the city, especially after dark, were bewildering. We had left behind the sounds of roosters, dogs, coyotes, bobcats, owls, crickets, and other animals moving freely through nature. Now we heard traffic and other foreign noises. The worst were the police and ambulance sirens. They reminded me of wolves. They conjured images of some sort of wild and dangerous screaming creature. Daylight brought little relief. Other boys and girls were out on the streets roller skating and riding bikes. They watched television and made nothing of talking on phone, which were all things that my siblings and I knew only through photographs. We were like Martians!"

Spirited Chief

Wilma's relocation to San Francisco challenged many of the traditional and cultural values that had made her so proud to be a Cherokee Indian. The family chose San Francisco because her maternal grandmother lived just ninety miles to the north. Wilma and her siblings would not have to endure the same boarding school humiliation and abuse that had left lasting scars on their father. But they were already experiencing their share of frustration, confusion, and disappointment about the public school system.

When Wilma entered the fifth grade, she discovered a deep racism from which she had been spared while living in an area populated by many Indians and children who shared her heritage and culture. "First of all," she notes, "Mankiller was not a strange name back home in Adair County, but it was a very odd name in San Francisco. The other kids teased me about the way I talked and dressed. It wasn't that I was so much poorer than the others; it was more that I was from another culture. My dad and brother worked long hours at a rope factory. The forty-eight dollars each of them brought home was never enough. My mom actually made clothes for us from potato sacks. One day, a lady on the street called her 'nigger lover.' The 'better life' the BIA had promised us was, indeed, life in a tough urban ghetto."

Wilma hated school and kept running away, trying to find refuge at her grandma's house in the country. She truly didn't want to live in the city, but she was finally able to come to terms with her distaste for her environment when her family moved to Hunter's Point in 1960. "It wasn't paradise; it was still a gang neighborhood with a lot of animosity between the black and Samoan youths. But we had a little house, and I was getting along pretty good with the black kids. My father had left the rope factory and was working as a longshoreman on the docks. He had also begun to supplement his income by playing poker. People would come to our house for poker games that lasted well into the night. Some of the men who played cards with him were men he worked with, but many were Native Americans he met at the Indian Center." Chief Mankiller's eyes brighten just naming the center.

"What I never found in schools, I found at the San Francisco Indian Center. I was a troublesome, unsettled teenager with no sense of direction, moody and self-absorbed. The Indian Center became an oasis where I could share my feelings and frustrations. It was a safe place to go, even just to hang out or watch television. It was located upstairs in an old frame building on Sixteenth Street, on the edge of the Mission district. We would jump on a bus and head for the Indian Center, the way some kids today flock to the shopping mall.

"It was important to everybody in my family, including my father. He ended up quitting his job at the docks and becoming a union organizer. He also spearheaded a project to establish a free health clinic for Indians living in the Bay Area. When he believed in something, he worked around the clock to get the job done. I inherited my dad's tenacity. Once I set my mind on something, I never give up. I was raised in a household where no one ever said to me, 'You can't do this because you're a woman, or because you're Indian or poor.' No one told me there were limitations. Of course, I wouldn't have listened to them if they had tried."

At the Indian Center, Wilma also met her first few boyfriends. "I didn't have a whole string of them. I was shy with boys. But there were a few who almost broke my heart. Rock 'n' roll and soul music helped mend it. I would listen to those hits and dream of the time I would be out of school and free. I still hated school, but I loved the Indian Center. And it was there that I first started feeling that some big changes were going to happen. Even before the 1960s cultural revolution, the Bay Area attracted artists and rebels who would act as merchants of change. Suddenly, a new generation was ready

133

Spirited Chief

to take over, and I was part of it. San Francisco was the place to be. Life started to be interesting again."

June 1963 was a month of violence and civil disobedience throughout the United States. In San Francisco, seventeen-year-old Wilma was fully aware of what was going on nationwide, but she also had something else on her mind. She had just graduated from high school. Big relief. She had also decided to move in with her sister, Frances. More freedom. And she was starting to fall in love. Big change.

"Once I was out of my parents' home, I had a taste of independence. I went right out to get a job. I had never entertained plans to go to college, so I found work and I felt good. That's where I was at in my life when I met Hugo in the summer of 1963. His full name was Hector Hugo Olaya de Biardi. I met him at a Latino dance. He was a native of Ecuador, four years older than me. He was charming and handsome, sophisticated and confident. Hugo had come to the United States on his own to pursue his academic goals. When I met him, he was studying business and accounting at San Francisco State University.

"Hugo was also worldly, somebody who had been around. To a ghetto kid like me, that was impressive. He took me places and introduced me to different types of music and cultures. We had a summer of pure fun. In October, I accepted his proposal to marry him. I was one month shy of my eighteenth birthday. My mother had run off at age fifteen to marry my father, so my parents could do little to oppose. We flew to Reno, my first plane trip, and got married. Then, since Hugo's father had presented us with one thousand dollars to be used for a wedding trip, we decided to go to Chicago. We were still in Chicago on Friday, November 22, when the television broadcasts announced the startling news that President Kennedy had been shot and killed that afternoon in Dallas."

134

When Wilma Mankiller looks back, she thinks 1963 was the real turning point in her life. Despite settling into her new role as a wife—and soon after as a mother, having become pregnant on her honeymoon—she also discovered that she was, like her father, suffering from kidney disease, an illness that she would have to battle for the rest of her life. "This brought about many changes in my daily existence, but I was billowing in the wind of social change that was blowing through America. Even before I had my second daughter in 1966, I started to feel restricted by the routine of the traditional wife. Experiencing what was going on around me in the culture was causing me to doubt whether or not Hugo and I would last.

"After the Watts Riots of August 1965 and March 1966 in Los Angeles, the conservative Republican Ronald Reagan was elected governor of California. Bobby Seale and Huey Newton founded the Black Panthers in October 1966. I could relate to their feelings and manifesto. Latinos were also starting to make their presence known; César Chávez successfully led rallies and strikes against California's major grape growers on behalf of the migrant workers. I could identify with them, too. I had worked on farms every summer during my teen years. I knew about the deplorable labor conditions.

"Then there were the civil rights proponents from middle-class America. President Lyndon B. Johnson's escalating involvement in Vietnam included shipping out more and more troops, as well as a growing number of students who did not want to take part in the Vietnam War. The University of California at Berkeley became the site of the Free Speech Movement. I was against the war and definitely for freedom of speech."

Meanwhile, the hippie movement was attracting school dropouts from all over America to the Victorian homes and streets of a San Francisco neighborhood called the Haight-Ashbury, where many rock musicians took up residence. "The Grateful Dead lived at 710 Ashbury, and the Jefferson Airplane lived nearby on Fulton Street. I would take my daughters for strolls over there and secretly wish to be part of that psychedelic, renegade culture. I decided to enroll in college. I had hated school, but I was starting to realize that education was an important part of leading an independent life. Once I became more independent, more active with school and community work, it became even more difficult to keep my marriage together. Before that, Hugo had viewed me as someone he had rescued from a miserable life. My newfound independence was threatening his role as my savior. But I wanted to set my own limits and control my destiny."

On November 8, 1968, Richard Nixon beat out Democrat Hubert Humphrey to become the thirty-seventh president of the United States. The following year, a political event even more important to Wilma than Nixon's election took place: the takeover of Alcatraz Island by a group of young Indian activists.

"It changed me forever. It gave me the focus I was searching for. In 1968, Clyde Bellecourt, a Chippewa from Minnesota, founded the American Indian Movement (AIM), which grew swiftly in popularity among young Indians. The Indian Center in San Francisco became a hotbed of insurrection. In November 1969, fourteen Native American youths—whose combined heritage represented more than twenty tribes— hitched a ride with a Sausalito yachtsman on a charter boat and seized the San Francisco Bay island that had once served as a prison called the Rock. Citing a forgotten clause in treaty agreements that said any unused federal lands must revert to Indian use, they claimed the twelve-acre island to attract public attention to the government's disrespect of treaty-related rights and its mistreatment of Indians."

In 1968, there had been a few improvements in the federal Indian policy. Congress had extended the protection of the

United States Bill of Rights to Native Americans, but it wasn't until the 1970s that Indians won the right to self-government and sovereignty and could finally rebuild their autonomous tribal governments.

Meanwhile, Alcatraz became a turning point in the lives of many more Indians, many of whom hadn't been previously politically active. "The cops kept chasing Indians away, but we would always find ways to get back. Sometimes the population on the island rose to one thousand. Before it was over, four of my brothers and sisters and their children had joined the original band. The occupation was incredibly successful and liberating for me. I have tried to retain that valuable experience, along with some of my youthful raw courage and idealism. I find it extremely helpful today as I continue to work for the revitalization of tribal communities."

It would take Wilma another ten years before she would return to her original tribal community. Her dad died during the Alcatraz standoff, and losing him was hard on the whole family. Wilma plunged even more deeply into her political commitment, studying law and treaty rights. She bought her first car without her husband's consent and realized how much she enjoyed making her own decisions. "Those were exciting years, and I met many interesting people. But despite all the opportunities there, I found my eyes turning away from the sea and the setting sun of the West. I was longing for the land of my youth, where the sun begins its daily journey. The circle had to be completed. I was getting ready to go home."

Wilma Mankiller returned to Oklahoma for good in the summer of 1977. She said her final goodbye to Hugo, whom she had divorced in 1974. She had resumed her family name immediately after the divorce, and three years later she was heading home, where her name had come from. Then she packed her daughters, their pet dog and guinea pig, and the family's belongings in a U-Haul truck and drove away from San Francisco.

"I would lie if I said coming back home was a bed of roses."

I'm sitting on the porch with Wilma in front of the frame house she built when she returned, just a hundred feet from the house where she lived as a little girl. She shares her home with her second husband, a Cherokee named Charlie Soap, and his son Winterhawk. Her daughters Felicia and Gina often stop by, and Wilma's widowed mother lives just down the road. To the north stand the Cherokee Hills, to the south the Cookson Hills, and the valley in between is a necklace of small farms, ranches, and fruit orchards, sassafras and persimmons, oaks, sycamores, and dogwood. Voices of jays, wrens, mockingbirds, and crows compose joyful serenades. Here is a woman who's in love with nature. She seems to have a love affair even with bugs and walking sticks. Insects crawl along the railing and over her legs, but Wilma limits herself to gently shaking them off or helping them to the redbud tree that grows near her porch.

"Not only did we not have money, but I didn't have a job when we got back. I had been exposed to a totally different culture in San Francisco, to Indian activism and liberated women. I came back to a place where the reconstituted tribal power was dominated by men. And I started thinking it was strange, since in ancient times women had a lot of power among Cherokees. They were the first to understand the necessity of planting crop fields close to camps, which changed agriculture and our nomadic way of life forever. Women chose the chief. They were never treated as simple assets of their husbands. They participated in all ceremonies and social events. They were in charge of distributing the food, and after wars they decided the destiny of prisoners.

138

"That was before the whites arrived, when war was mostly a game to show the bravery of young warriors—savage, even cruel sometimes, but without the political strings it later acquired. When I finally found my first job in 1977, working for the Cherokee Nation as a stimulus coordinator, women's opinions were held in very low regard. My job consisted of getting as many Indians as possible trained at the university level in environmental science and health, and then helping them reintegrate into their communities. It was a nice enough job title and well paying, but I was used to working in grass-roots democracy, and my nation seemed instead to be a huge bureaucracy."

Although disappointed by many things, Wilma reminded herself to be of good spirit, always emphasizing the positive instead of the negative. "When my then-boss discovered that I knew how to write grant proposals from my days in San Francisco, things started to change. By 1979, I was promoted to program development specialist. And when a couple of the grant proposals received funding and I started to earn some good revenue for the tribe, I came to the attention of Chief Swimmer and the council. Things were looking good. I decided to complete college by picking up a few remaining course credits at the nearby University of Arkansas in Fayetteville, an hour-and-a-half drive from my house."

Unfortunately, an unexpected tragedy awaited her on that road, one that would spoil more than Wilma's plans to go back to school. On November 9, 1979, she was driving her station wagon up the back-country roads to reach Highway 100. On the other side of the hill, a car headed for Stillwell pulled out to pass two other slow-moving cars. The driver couldn't see Wilma because of a blind spot, and she and Wilma crashed head on. Wilma's face was crushed, as was her right leg. Her left leg and ankle, as well as several ribs, were broken. The other driver sustained even more damage. She had a broken

139

neck and did not make it to the hospital in Tahlequah. Ironically, it turned out to be Wilma's best friend, Sherry Morris.

"I came to know that she was the other driver only weeks after the accident. Family and friends kept it from me, worrying that the truth could adversely affect my rehabilitation. I was struggling with many debilitating injuries. I stayed two months in the hospital and had to go back many times afterward. Before it was all over, I'd have to endure seventeen operations, mostly on my right leg. The doctors were considering amputation, since the chances were slim that I would ever walk again. I was determined to prove them wrong, despite the excruciating pain of being confined to a wheelchair with both my legs in full casts. I'm still not sure how I managed to regain mobility. But I did, dedicating more than one year and all my will power to my recovery process. In January 1981, I was finally able to return to my post with the Cherokee Nation."

Wilma went back to work charged with a new sense of purpose. She did not care to ascend the tribal hierarchy, but she did want to get things done, just like her father. She was named the first director of the Cherokee Nation Community Development Department, which grew under her direction. Wilma oversaw the development of an important project in the tiny, very poor community of Bell in Adair County. Without any funding, she managed to recruit an all-volunteer workforce to build a sixteen-mile water line and remodel several condemned homes. "In my mind," she offers, "the Bell project remains a shining example of community self-help, traditional sharing of physical tasks, and working collectively. The local residents served as their own labor force until grants were finally funded."

140   On a more personal level, the Bell community project is dear to Wilma because it was when she was working on it that she fell in love with her Cherokee husband. "Charlie Lee

Soap is a full-blood, hard-working Cherokee who shares my values, and he is probably the most well-adjusted male I have ever met. He has been my best supporter and has never felt threatened by my growing duties with the tribe. Our relationship stems from mutual respect and has become the strongest love I have ever known. We genuinely like each other. We never seem to get bored of one another, and we bring out each other's strengths."

Wilma's duties indeed grew when she was asked by Chief Swimmer to run as his deputy chief in the 1983 election. "It was a bold act, since he was a Republican and had been already challenged by many of his former supporters and political allies after being diagnosed with lymphatic cancer. They thought he was too ill to remain in office, but he wasn't the type to give up easily. So he bypassed his male friends to select me as his running mate.

"At first, I was scared and declined the offer. Because our tribe is so large, running for tribal office is almost like running for Congress. But I talked to Charlie, and he convinced me to give it more thought. In the end I accepted. I was still worried that most people would not like my ideas about grassroots democracy and my activist background. But I was wrong. Nobody challenged me on those issues, not once. Instead, all opposition to my candidacy would turn out to be because of one bare fact: that I am female.

"There were people saying that my running for office was an affront to God, and people saying that having a female run our tribe would make the Cherokees the laughing stock of the tribal world. There were death threats waiting for me in my mailbox, and I had the tires of my car slashed. I figured the best tactic was to ignore my denigrators. I built my campaign on a positive and cheerful foundation."

It worked. Wilma took office and rolled up her sleeves to show what a great leader was really made of. Then in September

141

of 1985, Chief Swimmer was asked by Ronald Reagan to serve as his Assistant Secretary of the Interior for Indian Affairs and to move to Washington, D.C., to head the BIA.

Article Six of the Constitution of the Cherokee Nation, ratified in 1976, specifies that the deputy principal chief automatically replaces the resigning chief. "I had to serve the balance of Ross Swimmer's term—from 1985 to 1987—without any real mandate from the people. It didn't feel too good. But I was determined to be a good chief. And I guess I was, since I was elected chief in my own right in 1987, when I made the decision to run on my own. At long last, I had the mandate I wanted: my own people had chosen me as principal chief of the Cherokee Nation. It was a sweet victory. Only after that win did I feel that the question of gender had been put to rest. Today I'm sure that if anyone asked members of our tribe if it really matters if the chief is male or female, the majority would reply that gender has no bearing on leadership. If I am to be remembered, I want it to be for my part in provoking this change of mentality."

EPILOGUE

In 1989, Wilma Mankiller underwent yet another surgery, hoping to resolve her progressing kidney disease by removing the cysts affecting both kidneys. It did not work, and kidney failure was imminent. Her only hope was finding a matching donor for kidney transplant.

Her daughters and sisters volunteered, but medical tests found them not to be suitable donors. Wilma's husband, Charlie Soap, called her older brother, Don, one of the two siblings who had remained in California. He was tested, and the results were good. Don donated one of his kidneys to his sister, enabling her to continue her life and work in good health.

In 1991, Mankiller decided to run for another four-year

142

term as chief. Her victory was a landslide, with 82.7 percent consensus from her people.

In 1995, Wilma Mankiller left office. She now dedicates her energy, expertise, and experience to implementing several projects that benefit the Cherokee Nation.

I'd rather take risks than regret I didn't dare to.

Professional Poker Queen

ANNIE DUKE

Annie Duke is the best all-around female poker player in the world today and recently achieved more fame than she ever expected to. She was already the leading money winner among women in World Series of Poker history and a familiar face for viewers of the show *Celebrity Poker* on Bravo. She was already the champion who had taken Hollywood star Ben Affleck under her wing and tutored him toward his $10,000 victory in the California State Poker No Limit Hold'em tournament at the Commerce Casino in June 2004.

Then in September 2004, Duke, a thirty-nine-year-old mother of four, beat out her older brother and mentor, Howard Lederer, a legendary poker player in his own right, and eight other poker champions for total winnings of $2 million and

145

first place in the World Series of Poker Tournament of Champions. The "Duchess of Poker" has achieved celebrity status herself. "Bold" and "beautiful" are words commonly used to describe her. She has become a regular in *People* and other "lowbrow culture" magazines—as her mom used to call them in an effort to divert Duke's attention to more serious reading during her teenage years.

Annie Duke is the first poker diva in history. But her path to professional gambling has been unusual.

Annie and her two siblings, older brother Howard and little sister Katy, were born in Concord, New Hampshire. They grew up on the campus of the local Saint Paul's School, where their father was a resident teacher of English literature and a language specialist. Annie, expected to follow in her father's footsteps, enrolled in New York's Columbia University, where she double-majored in English literature and psychology.

She went on to study cognitive psychology at the University of Pennsylvania and was the recipient of a National Science Fellowship. Though she felt stirrings of confusion and indecision about her future, she had always strived to live up to others' expectations and was very good in her field, so she continued. But just one month before she was to defend her PhD dissertation, her body gave her a clear signal that she should stop doing "the right thing." Annie had a vomiting fit that landed her in the hospital with a diagnosis of "extreme dehydration."

How did the future poker champion react to this turn of events? She called Ben—a friend from graduate school whom she had never even dated—and proposed marriage to him. She left her academic life then and there, without obtaining her PhD, and moved with him to Montana in 1992, where Ben's dad was living.

"We didn't have any money or any idea of what to do there," Annie tells me years later, when we meet face to face.

"But I'm kind of like Pollyanna: I always think things will work out."

But things actually didn't work out too well. Even raising the $125 for the mortgage every month was a problem. Though there weren't many jobs available in Montana, there were plenty of card games going on. And Annie knew how to play cards. In her family, intelligence was measured in terms of one's ability to play games as much as by academic achievement. And so it was in Montana, in the seedy, smoky backroom downstairs at the Crystal Lounge in Billings, that twenty-six-year-old Annie Duke started playing poker against cowboys, ranchers, and truck drivers.

I'd heard this legend long before meeting Annie for the first time in Las Vegas, Nevada, in the spring of 2000, during the World Series of Poker tournament.

Since the allure of gambling runs in my blood as well—with a lineage of card queens not to be outrivaled by my paternal grandmother, a national bridge champion and roulette addict—I was drawn to investigate the visibly increasing movement of women into the male-dominated world of poker. Annie Duke was considered the rising star of this trend. My first impressions of Annie in 2000 are still vivid.

I spot Annie at the downtown Horseshoe Casino—maybe the last family-owned casino in America. Located far from the frills of the Strip, the Horseshoe, which belongs to the Binion family, hosts the most lucrative annual gaming competition. The early May air outside is hot and thick as a blanket, but inside the casino everything is cool. Spectators' eyes are glued to the tables, where players keep their own eyes glued to their cards. Concentration surrounding a high-stakes poker game is intense and contagious.

Annie is holding her position at a table with players including Chris Ferguson and T. J. Cloutier, coauthors of several books about championship tournaments. Their books are

147

considered poker bibles, and players like these bet as much as $2,000 for antes (the bets posted before the hand starts) and $5,000 to $10,000 for blinds (the bets posted by the players sitting to the left of the dealer). At this level, there are only the fourteen players who have survived in a field that started with 512. They are divided into two groups, seven at each table. Annie is the only woman.

Long brown hair and reddish bangs cover her eyes, which, I imagine, are moving back and forth from the two cards in her hand to the others dealt on the table. Is she trying to calculate odds and guess what her opponents might be holding? Annie is sitting with one leg behind her, barefoot. They say it's her signature. She's visibly pregnant, thirty-eight weeks along, with her fourth child, a girl who they tell me will be called Lucy. There are $325,000 worth of chips in front of her.

The game starts, and in a matter of minutes, Annie drags reporter Jim McManus—sent by *Harper's Bazaar* to cover the event but infected by poker fever to the point of entering the game as a competitor—into a one-on-one match. The fact that he's made it to the finals is a shock even to him, and McManus makes history with this unusual turn of events.

"Play *me*, not the cards," is Annie's regular advice to her pupils when she imparts poker wisdom. Watching her in action, I wonder what she sees behind McManus's polarized shades. Is he a flirter, one of the two types, by Annie's account, that a woman player faces at a poker table? The second type is a chauvinist, and McManus isn't that. He's playing with a photo album of his family spread on his lap, a picture of his wife reading a book to their little girl as a good luck charm.

McManus shows kings. Annie has queens. The flop, the three cards dealt face up at the start of the game, comes up 2-7-ace, giving McManus a 43-2 probability to get the card he needs from the rest of the deck to beat her.

Adrenalin-juiced tension is peaking. So are the voices of

148

about fifty "railbirds," as spectator fans are called in poker jargon. They're cheering for Annie. They call her name loudly and invoke a third queen to save their girl.

But kings beat queens at least four times out of five. When "fourth street"—the fourth communal card, also called "the turn"—turns out to be the seven of clubs, Annie's fan club becomes hysterical, shouting for a queen. But "fifth street," or "the river," doesn't turn up the necessary queen. It turns out to be the jack of diamonds. Annie is suddenly down to $130,000.

She smiles bravely, but her cheekbones are flushed, her pupils dilated. Who knows Annie better than her baby sister, Katy Lederer, a poet and author who is working on a family memoir titled *Poker Face*? Katy is saying, to no one in particular, that Annie's pissed as the crowd gathers around to watch the action. This is a punch in the face of her competitive nature. When she was young—indoctrinated into the family love of games at a very early age—and playing Spit, Go Fish, or War in the family room, she was known to throw her cards in frustration anytime she didn't win.

She's a better player than McManus, no doubt about it, and poker is the only form of gambling in which sportsmanship, intelligence, bravado, and aggression—four skills for which Annie is renowned—count for more than sheer fortune.

This is still gambling, though. One day you win. One day you lose. Most days Annie wins. But the odds dictate that she must also lose once in a while.

"You've got to know when to hold 'em, know when to fold 'em," sings Kenny Rogers in the background. But Annie knows that even such an instinct isn't always enough. The wheel of fortune can't always spin in the same direction at the poker table, no matter how brave and skilled the players are.

A good day for Annie, up to this point, might bring winnings of up to $300,000. On worse days, she has lost up to

$100,000. She has been living in Vegas for four years now, having finally convinced her stay-at-home husband to move there from Montana. This way she can train at her "office" in the Bellagio casino every day, preparing for the big tournaments and championships. I've always wondered how somebody could actually *live* in Las Vegas, the air-conditioned, all-indoor city with its eternal soundtrack of coins sliding into slots that in turn eject hypnotic music, a spell broken only by the piercing sound of ambulances and police sirens that invariably erupt from the street, and amusement-park neon replicas of major landmarks from around the world.

I wonder how it's possible to raise children in this place. How does it feel to do mundane things here, like grocery shopping? Does money have the same worth in a place where so much of it changes hands in a split second? How do people with "normal" jobs, like waiters and store cashiers, feel? I have a hundred questions anytime I'm in Vegas. I am curious to know who the residents are of this mirage in the middle of the desert that is one of America's most rapidly expanding cities. I am curious about the habits of high-stakes rollers who come here to "vacation" on the shores of money-filled rivers. I am curious about people who make their living as professional poker players, too.

Annie's goal, I hear her saying to reporters afterward, is to send her four children, including the unborn girl she's carrying, to Columbia University with her earnings from gambling. Sarcasm laces her voice, since Annie has endured her share of disbelief that gambling could possibly be a viable career for a college-educated woman, and a Columbia University–educated one at that. Sarcasm is one of Annie's signature traits, the fifth "skill" she is notorious for.

150

As much as she's committed to playing and winning, her children come first. They are her absolute priority. "My kids fulfill my life," Annie is telling an interviewer after placing

ANNIE DUKE

tenth out of 512 entrants—the second-highest-ever finish by a woman—and taking home a prize of $52,000. "I'm proud of them because they breathe." It's clear that every calculated move at the poker table is driven by her desire to provide opportunities for her children. And when Annie had to choose between attending her daughter's sixth birthday party and participating in a tournament that could have netted her a six-figure profit, she chose the party.

"My brother said I could have paid for her college education that weekend. 'True,' I said, 'but when she's twenty-five and in therapy, she's going to be talking about how I missed her sixth birthday party.'"

Four years after seeing Annie in 2000, I contact her and ask to meet her again. I track her down through Ultimatebet.com and tell her about my book project. She gets back to me quickly. She's enthusiastic, encouraging, and honored to be included in my all-star collection of women who have lived their lives as an adventure instead of playing by the rules.

Since Annie is now living in Portland but also traveling all the time, we decide to meet in February 2005 in Los Angeles, where she'll be playing tournaments at the Commerce Casino.

"I need fifteen more minutes," a sleepy voice whispers into the phone receiver when I call Annie's room from the hotel lobby, twenty minutes past our appointment time. Having parked on the wrong side of the building, I have to cross the whole casino floor to reach the restaurant where we were meeting for breakfast. It is my first time in a poker-only casino, and I still can't get over the absence of the obnoxious cacophony that overwhelms the senses in Vegas or Indian reservation casinos. Silence, although pleasant, seems vaguely wrong.

Annie gets out of the elevator, apologizing by way of

151

explaining that she was up until three AM the night before. But she looks radiant and younger than when I saw her in Vegas almost five years ago. Since I last saw her, I've read her sister's memoir. I recall the warning their mom gave Katy when she expressed her wish to give a shot at a poker career herself: "I thought you'd be the normal one. I don't want another gambler in the family. Do you want to look like Annie and Howard? They look so ravaged at the end of the day."

It's still early, and Annie looks anything but ravaged. She's sporting pigtails and jeans that flatter her toned body. After four kids and approaching forty, she says she feels compelled to keep in shape. She's lost every bit of a Montana housewife's look and now resembles a hip model or actress with her good looks, which remind me of other women I've known who have a mixed heritage of Caucasian American and something else that contributes to a particularly unique appearance that people long to place. In my mind I speculate that she could be Irish and Native American, or some other interesting blend of cultures.

I tell her she looks amazing. "Actually," she confesses, "I'm obsessed with my weight. I go crazy when I gain five pounds. I hit the gym and work out like a maniac." It's a relief to know that even someone as self-assured as Annie has some obsessions, too, which she admits is actually a weakness. The thought of unwanted pounds piling up on her slender hips doesn't keep Annie from wolfing down a hearty brunch, though.

"I'm starving," she tells me as she eats. "I'm always hungrier when I have not slept enough." She confesses that she's been suffering from sleep deprivation since the birth of her first daughter, who's now ten. "When I retire, I want to sleep for a whole week," she proclaims. "I haven't slept more than a few hours each night in over ten years."

Nevertheless, Annie looks very awake and energetic to

152

me. She starts to tell me about the big changes in her life over the past few years. "I love living in Portland. It's so much nicer than Vegas. My house was built in 1904, and it's right in the historical center, surrounded by other beautiful old buildings. There is a sense of community, so it feels like a real neighborhood. To reach a Target or a Ross, I need to drive at least forty minutes, which says a lot. And for a single mom, as I am now, with young kids ages two to ten to raise, Portland is a much easier environment. I can't even imagine having teenagers going to high school in Las Vegas."

Annie had separated from her husband about a year before, after moving to Portland, and their divorce was finalized two months before we met this time. I'm surprised to hear this, since she always praised her husband for encouraging her career decisions and making them possible by staying home with the kids.

"It's true," Annie admits, "but there were big differences in character between us, and they grew bigger with time. Ben is a very negative person, just the opposite of how I am. He's often depressed, and it was really cutting into our relationship. I realized that all this was driving me away not only from him, but also from my kids. I was happier when I had to be gone for work than when I was home, because I didn't want to be around somebody who'd bring me down. Of course, one could say I knew how he was before. And I did, but I still tried to make our marriage work. I'm a Type A personality, so I took marriage vows very seriously. Only when I couldn't deny any longer that I was becoming a different person, one I liked less, did I decide to file for divorce."

I ask her how she manages now, with the kids and her traveling. "I have a full-time, live-in nanny and a personal assistant. Plus, I'm trying to be friends with my ex-husband, to deal with the kids' issues together. He lives in Los Angeles, but he also has a house in Portland, so he can take the kids

153

when I'm out of town. He's pretty good at that. It's very help-ful in months when I'm away playing tournaments for four-teen days, which I will be next February, or even worse next March, when I'll be away from home for twenty days."

I wonder how Annie's kids feel about her job. What do they tell their classmates? How they deal with such a dif-ferent kind of mom? "They love to brag that their mom is a famous poker champion, but they don't like the traveling part. I guess they have the same issues that other sports champions' kids have."

Annie likes to compare poker to sports. She believes unequivocally that poker is the only sport in which women can compete with men on equal footing. "There is a pretty big physical component to almost any competitive sport, and men are bigger and stronger in their bodies. But in poker, I can compete against men and be on the same level. At the table, I consider myself a player, not a woman. As a matter of fact, I'm incredibly offended by women-only tournaments, because to me, poker is all about the mind."

Annie gets passionate about this topic, even though she has been widely criticized about it. There have been rumors about her being a snob. People say she despises women-only tournaments because she feels superior to other women. But that's not where she's coming from.

"It's like telling women they can't compete against men at the same level with their minds. Isn't that offensive? It's the equivalent of saying women are dumb. There is only one very good reason for ladies' tournaments: to introduce women to a game, which is wonderful, a really great way to exercise the mind. And gambling is a male-dominated world, so it can be difficult for women to come in and sit at a table with men without feeling intimidated. But those ideas aren't valid on a very competitive, professional level."

Intellectual challenges have always turned Annie on.

154

ANNIE DUKE

"That's my family heritage. The message was that if you keep a sharp mind, you will succeed in anything you set out to do. It inspires a lot of confidence."

A man stops at our table to congratulate Annie and shake her hand. He says that there is a questionnaire this month in a poker magazine that asks readers, "What do you think Annie Duke represents in the poker world?" Over half of the responses to the multiple-choice replies have been that Annie Duke is the best woman player of all time. She's pleased by the news, and she's not shy about her popularity.

"When I happened to win the World Series of Poker Tournament of Champions main event last September," Annie recalls, "which fell on the same day as the ladies' final, I noticed that many people, mostly men, were offended by my choice to enter the main event. *Annie Duke has slapped women in the face* was the vibe I was getting. *She's saying, 'I'm better than you.'* They felt like I insulted women. And I was like, *What are you talking about?* Because I'm the one who's taking the feminist stand? I was saying to women that they can play with the big boys and don't need to be separated. That's the beauty of poker.

"Another great thing about poker as a sport is that you can be as good in your fifties as you were in your thirties. It's a game you can play for life. There is no age limit. And this, too, is great for women who, many times, face age discrimination in other fields. So why limit yourself and accept gender discrimination? It's supposed to be a world championship, meaning that every person living in the world can compete in it. If I won a bracelet in a ladies' event, I'd throw it in the trash. It would be meaningless to me because it doesn't invite everyone in the world to participate. It invites women only."

When Annie started playing poker in Montana, she faced more than gender discrimination. "I was very young. I wiggled my way into this back room in a bar, where I was told

155

Annie in action at the table.

there were games going on. I had to go downstairs and swim through a cloud of smoke. The average age in there was fifty-five or sixty. They were a bunch of ranchers who didn't want to let me in. Those people would go to play poker to get away from their wives, and this girl shows up. And not only am I sitting there all talkative and giggling, but I'm taking their money. I'd get horrifically bad reactions and insults."

They called her "pussy." They called her "cunt." She was constantly confronting name-calling.

"The insults were bad, very sexually oriented. But I was like, 'Hey, you can call me whatever you want, but you're not going to hurt my feelings.' My strength lay in the fact that I didn't take any of their insults personally," says Annie. "My revenge was winning their money."

Annie needed money to pay her mortgage, and she didn't

156

have many other ways to get it. She didn't want to work as a waitress. She couldn't be a professor or college teacher, since she had dropped out of graduate school, and she was married to somebody who wanted to live in Montana. Poker seemed the best solution to her problems. Her brother Howard agreed and backed her up with $2,300 to get her into the game on the professional circuit.

"I was going to the Crystal Lounge, commuting forty-five minutes every day in the car, just as if I were going to an office job. It was all business for me from the start. I had to get myself ready before going into a casino. Preparing myself to not allow them to treat me like a sex toy or not like an equal. It took some guts."

My personal experience of traveling through Montana by myself, a woman alone with a California license plate, tells me Annie is right. I'm not saying all men are macho in Montana, but there is no shortage of them, either. They're not so used to independent, assertive women, and they often feel threatened. Putting women down is their defense mechanism, helping them avoid facing their own fears.

"My family played a big part in my courage," Annie tells me. "They let me be competitive and daring, making me feel confident about it. Every day I was encouraged to be aggressive. And we were always expected to do well. So it was like, 'Look, Mom, I got all As!' and the response was, 'Of course you got all As, because you're a member of this family.' But it was worth the trade, since in this society not many women are encouraged to be smart. It can be considered detrimental to your dating career." Annie is very happy that her daughter is growing up in a place and time where the mentality is more open. "She's only ten, but she's already a feminist."

I ask Annie if she plays cards with her kids. "Not the way my parents used to play with us. Games in my family were the main, and often the only, interaction I had with my parents. I've had cards in my hands since I was born. We never played poker, but we played other games. And not only cards, but any and every type of game that makes you use your mind, like Monopoly. I play Monopoly with my kids, too. It's a great intellectual exercise."

She shifts the conversation back to Montana and the beginning of her poker-champion career. "All those nasty, rude men in Montana didn't discourage me. They made me want to play even more, and to beat them even more. I had a fire burning in me to take every one of those nasty guys' money."

This is another big difference that I've considered between poker and other kinds of gambling, like roulette or slot machines: The money you win is other people's money, not the house's. Therefore, poker can breed competition and fire up anger, since it can sometimes feel better to play and win against someone you don't like. But this can go the other way, too, when a player might care about the person they are playing against and ultimately beat.

"The first one to turn to poker in our family was my brother. He had gone through a lot of ups and downs on the poker circuit, and I had seen him use up all his college funds in his twenties, when he wasn't a very good player. Then he got very big and started playing in the big tournaments, some of which were really sleazy, and at gross clubs where there were a lot of drugs."

Howard went to New York at first and, while trying his hand at poker, started a parallel career as a bookie, during which he employed their own mother—who had also left New Hampshire and her husband to go to New York and pursue her acting dream—to run numbers in the betting game.

"I've seen the underbelly of gambling," Annie continues, "and I'm happy that my brother pulled himself out of it. I knew

ANNIE DUKE

I could make money at it, but I didn't necessarily think it was a positive career. The money Howard lent me was enough to keep me going in the Montana games for a while. I started playing and winning, and I also won my brother's admiration. He invited me to go to Las Vegas, where he had recently relocated. He encouraged me to try playing in tournaments, and I made $70,000 in winnings the first year."

Howard was the person most pleased with Annie's success. "He had this dream for me to become the best female player in the world. Mine was just to pay the bills. I was less concerned with success and popularity, and that's still the case. I don't really care about what anybody thinks. I care about what's happening in my life and whether I'm happy and have enough money to live. But I don't have super-fancy cars or a luxurious house, or a top-of-the-line stereo system or plasma TV, because I don't really need those things. I am not jealous. I don't compare what I have to what other people have. It sounds silly to me. It's so obviously senseless, because it's impossible to succeed at being the person who has the most. There will be always be somebody richer or nicer looking. So when my brother was telling me about his vision, I was like, 'Yeah, whatever!'

"But I am happy to give him credit at this point. We have a great relationship. I knocked him out of the World Series Tournament, but it could have gone exactly the other way, and that would never ruin our relationship. My brother has always been proud of my achievements."

It's rare to find two siblings so accomplished in the same field. "We are both among the best ten players in the world, so the opportunity to compete against each other comes along pretty frequently. People consider poker a bankable annuity, but what matters to me is the enthusiasm, the fascination. I feel eager every day to learn more about this game. So does Howard. I am happy when people

159

Professional Poker Queen

are interested in us for our personalities, because that is what is behind our success."

Annie's personality has always been very strong, but that did not spare her from the troubles she ran into growing up. "The other day I was talking to my daughter, who's having problems making friends at her new school. She feels like she's not fitting in, and I was trying to explain to her that her differences can be good. In elementary school, I didn't know how to relate to my peers. It was only in college that I finally made some friends. In elementary school, I was teased incessantly because I was not amused by or interested in the same things kids my age were into. Maybe I grew up too early because I was so stimulated at home. But in the end, being pushed beyond my limits was a very good thing for my life. And now I have tons of friends.

"'But that's because you're a famous poker player,' my daughter said. And I said, 'No, I am a famous poker player because of who I am.' And I also explained to her that my life would be equally interesting whether people take notice or not. I became famous when people started recognizing me because I was on TV, but I was playing poker for ten years before I started appearing regularly on television.

"So my message to my daughter is the same my parents gave me: Whatever you choose to do, put your heart into it, and whether people notice or not, you'll end up living quite an extraordinary life." I'm also trying to educate my kids about the idea that money is important, but it's not everything. In a business like mine, money comes and goes. One day you're rich; the next you can be broke. But I take my parenting responsibilities very seriously. With four kids to bring up and send to college, I need to manage my money with care. In my day-to-day life, I have more anxiety about dropping $500 on a dress than I do about using the same amount for a bet. But the difference is that with the purchase of the dress, the $500

160

is gone; on a bet, I earn equity. Investing money in poker is, to me, a better bet than investing in the stock market."

I'm wondering how such a serious attitude about money reflects the way Annie plays at the poker table. How can she feel relaxed and calm enough to keep up her poker face, unreadable by her opponents, when she pushes forward thousands of dollars in chips on a bluff? "I always try to use my tools the best I can, and the secret to it is to first understand the nature of the tools you're using. When you play, your chips don't represent money, they represent power, and you're trying to move them in a way that accomplishes your goal, which is getting other people's chips."

Her sister Katy's memoir recalls a dialogue between Katy and the psychiatrist for whom she was working at the time. One day the doctor tells Katy that mainstream theory holds that all gamblers are masochists. Katy can't believe her ears, since her experience tells her the contrary. "No way!" she says to the doctor. "My sister is a sadist. Freud must be wrong. Annie wants to subjugate and dominate everybody else when she plays. She's not a masochist."

"I know the value of the dollar," Annie continues, "and I am very aware of the necessities of a big family like mine. But I approach poker as a business. When I sit at the table, I cannot be scared of using my money to advance toward my goals. Even in the beginning, I paid for my entrance fee for the first tournament with $600. That was a lot of money for me then, but I couldn't think like that, or I wouldn't have been a good competitor. You can't sit at a poker table with fear in your baggage."

I'd like to know what Annie fears. I'm curious about her ability to take risks in other situations in life. "Let's put it like this: I like to fly, but I wouldn't go bungee-jumping. I'm an optimist. I always think things will turn out just fine in the end. I make a lot of impulsive decisions, like proposing to

161

Professional Poker Queen

my husband, a guy I had never even kissed. We were just old college friends!"

She gets deeper into self-analysis. "I'm very competitive and ambitious, and I'm very laid back about how other people behave, but not about myself. I am forgiving only to others. I'm very hard on myself. I am self-assured, but I have insecurities."

What can Annie's worst insecurity be? Her worries are surprisingly normal. "I obsess about my weight, and I have issues about getting old," she laughs. "Yes, I know it's silly, and that's where I feel like I'm such a chick. I wasn't brought up to believe that my worth is based on what I look like, but that doesn't mean I don't care. I think people my age have more difficulties with this issue than our mothers, maybe even because there are many so-called remedies around, so you almost feel guilty if you age before your friends do. I am pushing forty, which is the age a lot of iconic figures I grew up with were, like the mom in *Happy Days*, who was only forty but so matronly! That's what it is: I don't want to look matronly. So I work out obsessively, but I still have it stuck in my head: *You're forty, you're done*. That's how it was for women for a long time, and it's only just starting to change. But mainly what's changing is that we have more tools to make people forget that we're forty, or to make them reconsider what forty means."

Of course, Annie knows perfectly well that she does not look forty, or matronly, for that matter. "Right. People don't even come close to guessing my age. I get compliments all the time. But that doesn't change the way I feel. I've gotten to the point where, when people ask my age, I don't want to answer. It's a hang-up of mine that I despise. And being in the spotlight means that everybody knows every detail of your life, so you can't have any secrets. Plus, I can't even use Botox for wrinkles," she finally gives in, "because it would compro-

162

mise my sarcastic expression, something I am very fond of. So I guess I'll be forty and break new ground at the poker table, showing the men that I'm not done. And then I'll be fifty and sixty, and I'll never be done!"

This is pure Annie, all bravery and nonconformity. This is the reason why I sought her out for this book. I was eager to include her in my collection of life stories of women who choose to live by their own standards, Annie's personality is a mix of enthusiasm and love for challenges. But she also has a great sense of humor that allows her to take nothing too seriously, not even herself. And that is why she'll be always able to sustain her invincible spirit, which is usually reserved for people in their younger years, no matter how old she gets.

EPILOGUE

A book about Duke's life is in the works, followed by a movie. She also has plans to appear in a sitcom and is working simultaneously on two other TV show ideas and doing endorsements for four DVDs about poker. All of this is in addition to her ongoing consulting for Ultimatebet.com, an online card room where she teaches poker skills and plays live against subscribers.

There are millions of ways to spice up your life, even if you don't feel like you need a radical change.

How to Live a More Reckless Life

♀ ♀ ♀

You don't need to be a self-defined kick-ass woman to put a little bit of recklessness into your life. You don't need to live outrageously 100 percent of the time for your entire life. It's certainly not a requirement that you be single, nor are you excluded from recklessness if you have children. (If you have a partner and children, you might even need a little bit more recklessness in your life! In fact, they can be part of your unconventional lifestyle, or they can learn to respect that little space or part of your life that you claim as your very own.)

Adding recklessness to your life is very much like trying out a new recipe—you mix in a spice that you've never tried before. You start with just a pinch, and taste what it does to the overall effect. And then if you like it, you add a little more. And if you don't, you keep on trying new flavors.

There are millions of ways to spice up your life, even if you don't feel like you want or need a radical change. Maybe your life is just as fabulous as a peach pie in the summertime—it tastes exactly like you expect, and you don't really want anything different. But what if there are new adventures just around the corner from your house, in a part of your neighborhood you haven't yet explored? Should you ignore all the potential that changing your patterns could result in just because you find comfort in knowing exactly what your perfect peach pie is supposed to taste like?

Little things that can bring recklessness to your life are as simple as shopping in the ethnic foods section of your local market to try out a new recipe from your Mexican or Indian or Chinese cookbook; it's the same market, just a different aisle. Pick the kids up from school and take a different route home. Take them on an unexpected trip to the beach or an interactive museum. It's all about the way you live your life. See what it feels like to be a kid yourself. Try to recover that playful attitude children have. Have you ever noticed how kids get excited by novelty? Be excited yourself. Take the young ones to the zoo with an attitude of exploration and curiosity. Have fun and let your imagination run wild. Hear the sounds of the jungle, smell the scent of Africa in the middle of the city. . . . No kids and no zoo in your life? No problem! Enroll in a dance class; salsa or flamenco will do wonders for your body and your mood. But you don't like exercise at all? Try learning a new language. Buy a course cassette or CD that you can listen to during your commute to work. Rent foreign movies from countries that you've always fantasized about going to. It's all about bringing a little bit of the unknown into your daily routine.

Maybe these suggestions aren't enough to quench your thirst of discovery and longing for *big adventure*. You don't have to be the kind of woman who'd circumnavigate the world solo on a sail boat to have a grand adventure, though. Make a reservation for a bed-and-breakfast in a town not too far from your home. Book a trip that is supported by an organization if you're a person who's looking for companionship or looking for someone else to take care of coordination and hassles.

You might think this is easier said than done, but it doesn't have to be. With this "alphabet" of steps, you'll have all the inspiration and knowledge to actually *do it*. The list of websites, books, and organizations that follows will help you along your path to becoming a little bit more of a reckless woman. You'll be amazed to discover how much is out there to help you get started.

• A IS FOR AWARENESS •

Be adventurous by being aware. Awareness is the most important corollary to adventure. Risk taking becomes a lot less scary if you cultivate your ability to be aware—not only of your emotions, though very important, but also of your surroundings. Be mindful of the reactions that your actions cause. Be aware of the reasons why you make a choice. It's not about overanalyzing your behavior. It is about cultivating a different kind of attention not often used in daily life and avoiding the automatic response. The more you try to be aware the more it becomes natural to you—and the more you'll feel like you can trust your gut instinct.

I personally do a lot of things that are perceived as "risks" according to other people's standards, yet I don't feel scared taking them. Why? Because I'm aware of what's involved in those risks, of my possible reactions, and of the possible pitfalls. For instance, I love walking in the darkness at night, and oftentimes I'm alone. That might sound more nutty than adventurous, but it strengthens my courage in my daily life

167

and makes my sight, both physical and intuitive, sharper. But I'm also careful to choose *where* I walk alone at night. I never go walking in places that I haven't seen in the daylight or checked out at night first in a car or with others so that I can assess the safety of the area. I don't advise women to go out and walk alone in places they're not sure are safe, especially in wooded or canyon areas, but I do suggest going with a friend and splitting up enough so that you can feel like you're alone at least for a short while. Take your dog. Be aware and be flexible. This kind of awareness has saved me in many of my adventures and given me more confidence and self-reliance.

· B IS FOR BODY ·

You can be reckless no matter how much you weigh or what your body mass index is. You can be reckless if you're overweight or athletic, short or tall. Just as you can be sexy no matter what the scale says, recklessness comes in all shapes and sizes. The myth of the necessity of a "perfect body" is actually the first thing you need to get rid of on your quest to bring more recklessness into your life. What you really need is to feel good *in* your body, knowing that you can count on it to support you in your adventurous pursuits. How do you make your body happy? "Train" it to respond to your requests by rewarding it every time your body promptly answers them. Let's say you want to increase your endurance and walk a longer distance than you're accustomed to. While walking, focus on the vanilla-scented hot bath that you'll reward yourself with as soon as you get home. And when you do get home, indulge in your well-earned relaxation time. This way, you create a fabulous connection between your body and mind.

Reckless

This "natural understanding" comes from a chemistry that scientists have investigated for a long time. Expectation of a reward activates endorphins in your brain, and endorphins circulating through the blood are a powerful nutrient that feeds feelings of joy and satisfaction. That's what you want from your body.

Which kind of rewards should you provide? That's a very personal choice, and you can have fun experimenting with different kinds. See and feel what each one of them do to your body and mind.

• C IS FOR CHALLENGE •

I love challenges. If one of my friends wants me to do something, they know that if they frame it as a challenge then I'll bite on it. But not everybody feels this way. If you don't, though, you'll still be faced with many challenges throughout your existence. So you need to get friendly with them. Focus on the positive part. Focus on the opportunity challenge provides, not only if and when you overcome the obstacles and achieve victory, but in each step of the process. The journey is definitely the destination. Think about it as a game—basketball or chess or whatever you're into. You will need strategy. Intuition. Common sense. Courage. Maybe other skills depending on what your talents are. Just forget about fear. No matter how big the challenge is, you'll feel fabulous just by going for it rather than rejecting it because you let fear freeze your desire. I certainly haven't won all the challenges I've embraced. Neither did the outrageous women I profile in this book. But what makes these women outstanding is that they went for the challenge despite not knowing the outcome. I have never blamed myself for not achieving the best possible result. I feel confident in knowing that I can

169

only achieve *my* best possible result, and that I always try my hardest and use all of my talents and resources. That's all that matters.

• D IS FOR DREAMING •

You have an entire adventure park waiting for you every night. All of us dream even if we don't remember. And if you don't remember, there are tricks that can help you start remembering. It's worth the effort since dreams can provide you with lots of incredible adventures in other realms. You might say, "But my dreams are not adventurous, I dream about things that happen to me in my everyday life." But things that look similar or seem like your daily experiences might actually look completely different in your dreams if you pay close attention to details. It is possible to learn how to roam around more in your dreams, exploring new territories and even new terrain, like the sky or water, in dreams where you fly like a bird or swim like a dolphin. Aboriginals say that all our creation has been dreamt before ever materializing itself. Read about what dreaming represents in our culture. Most native peoples and tribal cultures pay great respect to dreams and turn to their dreams in making important decisions. There are tons of books about dreaming, from manuals to very entertaining storytelling. Read them before going to bed and you may start to pick up tips and skills that will help you make dreaming more a part of your life.

• E IS FOR ENTHUSIASM •

If you're feeling bored, tired, or depressed, try enthusiasm for a change. I know this might sound Pollyannaish if you're in a bad mood, but all you have to do is give it a try and see how it makes you feel. Remember, even in the most difficult or use-less situation, there is always a silver lining. Think of some-thing that diverts your attention, something that you know will make you feel excited if you let yourself. Ayun Halliday shares how she was able to make the best out of remedial, meaningless jobs in her book *Job Hopper*. "Think about it this way," she says. "You're stuck in an office Xeroxing all day, just you and the Xerox machine. But with all that time on your hands, you can have the most extraordinary, secret, imaginary sex life!" The same can be true in your dealings with people. Let your imagination take hold, add just a bit of enthusiasm to an old and worn out relationship, and see what you get—probably an enthusiastic response. Put some enthusiasm into cleaning the house, maybe experimenting with new products while listening to an exciting soundtrack to pace your efforts. It will become a lot easier, and you can look forward to bor-ing tasks with a lot less dread. Remember Mary Poppins and her "spoonful of sugar" recipe for helping the "medicine go down"? It does work. As long as you believe it and put some enthusiasm into it.

• F IS FOR FORTITUDE •

To be reckless, you need to develop a certain kind of strength, which is more than physical stamina or muscular power. For-titude is the word used by the Lakota-Sioux people to indicate the second of the four necessary virtues to live a good life. (The others are Bravery, Generosity, and Wisdom.) Fortitude is strength of character and the ability not to be crushed by failure. Failure—thanks to the new economy—is not a stigma anymore, even in the business world. Smart company own-ers say that they prefer to hire people who've experienced failure because it tells them that these people have failed and

171

recovered. They have not been destroyed by failure. These are people who learned from their mistakes and got back on their feet. One very good way to develop fortitude is to not take yourself too seriously. Add a bit of humor to something that on its surface might feel like tragedy, and it will become more bearable.

• G IS FOR GEAR •

Whatever the adventure you want to plunge into might be, you need to have the right equipment. This does not mean spending a bunch of money to buy the best possible winter clothes for a trip to Alaska. It means being aware of the needs you'll face no matter what your adventure and being equipped to solve any possible problems or challenges that arise. Part of this involves preparedness and understanding what you're getting yourself into. Let's say you want to learn how to climb. It's great exercise that develops mind-body connection, involves strategy, and gives great satisfaction both mentally and physically. You can start small, without even buying ropes and hooks, though you do need a good pair of climbing shoes. You can buy them slightly worn. People go through them quickly when they advance to the next level. Post something on Craigslist (www.craigslist.org) to see if anybody wants to donate you a pair. But don't start climbing without them or you'll put yourself at risk more than is necessary. Knowing the importance of your gear is essential.

• H IS FOR HELP •

Whatever your adventure, you need help. No matter whether you're thinking about traveling solo or starting your own business. By reaching out and sharing your goals, doubts, hopes, and fears with others, your concerns will immediately become less overwhelming. Even if you are a solitary and self-reliant person, you still need help. You can find help in many places. Books, libraries, organizations, on the Internet . . . even in unexpected places, such as radio shows or documentaries about and by people doing things you admire. One woman told me how she got funds to finance her project just because she happened to talk about it on the air after calling in to answer a question in a musical contest. Somebody listening found her idea appealing, called the radio show to get her information, and, in a matter of a few days, she had an investor for her business idea. Be resourceful and creative, and also open to help from unexpected places. Get yourself all the help you need to feel more confident.

• I IS FOR INTIMACY •

This is a tough one. People can be very reluctant to share intimate thoughts or feelings if they don't know you very well, and sometimes not even when they do know you well. Unwillingness to be open and share on any level results in communication becoming predictable and uninteresting. Choose to be daring. Be intimate with people even upon first meeting. As the women profiled in this book did with me, share personal details and let your experiences be known. To let somebody "in" means sharing your intimate thoughts and feelings. That is a great gift and it will not go unnoticed. You'll be surprised at the rewards you'll get in return. Don't know how to do it? Read some women's blogs (or some men's). There are many bloggers who are able to share very intimate reflections with whomever happens to come across their blogs online. Try www.barlowfriendz.net by John Perry Barlow, cofounder of Electronic Frontier Foundation. He's a

173

former lyrics writer for the Grateful Dead and the man is a genius who talks about politics, economy, and other serious issues with intelligence and wit. But the reason why I love him is his ability to "strip naked" in front of many. Sometimes he's shameless and he exposes his feelings and emotions by making you feel a part of his life even when he's unreachable, traveling, or working in Brazil. If you don't know where to start looking for blogs, try browsing the small list I include in the resource section at the end of this book. And check out the Reckless blog (www.be-reckless.com), where you can post your intimate reflections and share them with other reckless—or wannabe reckless—women.

• J IS FOR JOY •

Sheer joy is an incredible force. Children are joyful, able to fully enjoy even the smallest pleasures in life. You can allow yourself to savor the joy of a moment even when you're worried, sick, or sad. It will actually help you ease the pain. It will help you not to get stuck and frozen in any situation. The most common expression of joy is smiling. Try smiling more often. You'll be surprised that smiling actually works to make you feel happier. People respond in unexpected and wonderful ways to people who are quick to smile. Smile with your eyes, too, not just your lips, and see how it makes you feel better even when you're sad.

• K IS FOR KARMA •

Karma is a very interesting Buddhist concept that describes one's individual destiny. As much as I love the concept, I have to admit that I've had trouble accepting that karma exists independently from an individual's will. I believe that a person is lucky to find her calling in this life, but I am of the mind that much of this is wrapped in a person's willpower and sense of personal ambition. I see karma as an evolution of events that can take this or that turn depending on the steps we choose in moving down the path toward our goals. Ultimately, I believe that everybody is the arbiter of his/her own destiny. So my advice is this: Determine your own karma. Do it gently and according to the laws of nature and spirituality. It will feel right and it will make you happy if you're aware of the subtleties of karma and that it exists as a positive energy to be tapped into if you choose to be open to it.

· L IS FOR LOVE ·

Romance is just a part of love. You don't need romance to be reckless, but you can certainly be reckless in romance. Falling in love is almost always reckless. Today you can look for romance everywhere, in the most nontraditional places. Consider online dating if that's where you want to start your next adventure. Or heat up your existing relationship by trying new things with a partner you've been with for years. The important thing about romance is to believe that anything is possible, and to consistently put effort into making things fun and different, even if it's only once a month. In cultivating love, strive to have the attitude that, no matter what comes to mind, you can say, Why not? When I asked Beatrice Wood, a great artist who happily lived to 105, what her secret to longevity was, she grinned and told me: "A healthy diet of young men and a little chocolate every day." Whether she was really dating young men up until old age is between her and those young men, but what struck me about her was her fun attitude toward love, or the possibility of love, which was on par with that of women one-fifth her age.

175

How to Live a More Reckless Life

• M IS FOR MUSIC •

Music inspires recklessness. There is nothing like music to put you in the mood. Try music that makes you feel hopeful, brave, happy . . . invincible. For me that means Jimi Hendrix (all his music is "Bold as Love" to my ears) and The Doors (a song for all, "Light My Fire"). How about also "Ride of the Valkyries" by Wagner, the epic "Alive" by Pearl Jam, and the high-adrenaline energy of Red Hot Chili Peppers? And let's not forget about Sinead O'Connor and the band Cat Power. And what about movie soundtracks? There's *The Last of the Mohicans*, by Trevor Jones and Randy Edelman, or *The Phantom of the Opera*, by Andrew Lloyd Weber. I could go on and on. But everybody has different tastes. Create your recipe for your own reckless soundtrack accordingly. Listen to it when you're overwhelmed or doubtful. Music will sweep your moods away. Music will make you dance and transport you to another place. Music can bring recklessness to your everyday routine.

• N IS FOR NOTHING •

Abolish that word from your vocabulary. "Nothing" does not exist. There is always something going on, something to look forward to, something else to try. Alternatively, make peace with "nothingness." Don't be scared by emptiness. It is a necessary state. As the book of the I Ching teaches us, life goes in circles. When you pour water in a vase, you can only fill it to the top. If you want to fill it more, you have to empty it first. When something is unbalanced, it already has the "seed" of balance in it, ready to turn and transform. Understanding how life is broken into millions of temporary states of being will help you understand that all states of

176

being, even void, are necessary parts of living, as long as you understand that every aspect is temporary and shifting to make space for the next state of being.

• O IS FOR OR •

The existence of "or" in our vocabulary means that there's always another possibility. "Or" is there to open your eyes to things outside of your scope of vision, outside of your aware-ness. "Or" is the flexibility to consider other possible inter-pretations or solutions. Nothing in this world is either totally black or totally white. Consider the drop of white in the black half of the symbol of the Tao, the black in the white. This is symbolic of the "or" that exists in each space and helps inform our lives in a way that encourages seeing things for more than they appear. If you invite the possibility of "or" into your life, then your trained eyes will automatically scout the ground for other potential avenues when it seems like the road is blocked. And they will do so effortlessly.

• P IS FOR PASSION •

This is my favorite word, not only in the Reckless Alphabet, but in the whole vocabulary. I'm attracted to people who have passion for something. I don't care what it is that ignites their fire, as long as they have that fire in them. Most of us have many passions, and some of us have to put our passions to the side because we are swamped by the hectic pace of our daily lives. Recover that passion. Dig it out. Give your passion some breathing space. Go for. It is never, *never* too late. Maybe you're longing to get into ceramics or acting, but are held back by what other people might say or because you wonder if it's a waste of time. It's not frivolous or less important than any other

177

priority in your life. Don't make excuses for *not* starting a new hobby. Just do it. For your own pleasure and enjoyment. It will make you feel lively.

• Q IS FOR QUESTION •

Don't hold back. Ask all the necessary questions to satisfy your curiosity and make you feel confident before throwing yourself into any endeavor, whether it be an adventure, business enterprise, or relationship. That does not mean interrogating somebody and then being judgmental of their answers. Asking questions is totally legitimate and even appreciated when the asking person is perceived as open-minded, curious, and authentically interested to know the answer. But there is an art even to asking questions. Be direct but polite. Ask in a kind manner. Don't corner the person you are asking. Let her feel free to take the time she needs to think your question over before responding. That way the Q&A will become more dialogue and less precinct interview.

• R IS FOR ROSES •

Remember to stop and smell the roses, but also remember to relax along the way. My suggestion is that you bring more roses into your life and home. I'm partial to roses because they're so delicate and fragile and yet, at the same time, they have thorns. I like that contradiction. But other flowers work too. When I went to India for the first time, I was amazed by the beauty and grace of the women—all of them, whatever their age or shape. I wondered what it was that made them seem like princesses in my eyes. Then I noticed one small detail. They all wore a fresh flower in their hair. Even the poorest woman would stop at the market every morning to

178

buy a fresh flower and put it into her hair. It was the smallest touch that made me pause and consider their attentiveness to the simple beauty that a small flower could bring to their everyday lives.

• S IS FOR SILENCE •

Silence is necessary sometimes. Silence is rejuvenating and nourishing. Don't be afraid of silence. When the noise of the external world and your internal dialogue stop, that's when you can listen to the spirit world, including your own spirit. When I can stay silent with somebody, when I don't feel pushed to fill any void in the conversation, that tells me that I am able to feel truly comfortable with that person. None of us needs to talk; we talk because we have something to say. We live in a very noisy world. Allow yourself some silent pauses from your talking. It will clear your mind and relax your body.

• T IS FOR TRUST •

If you want to be reckless, you need to be trusting of yourself and of others. This is a concept I can't emphasize enough. Be trusting regardless of all the disappointments you have inevitably accumulated throughout your life. Being trusting does not mean naively throwing yourself into anything without checking it out. But it does mean not having assumptions or prejudices. The more you develop your gut instincts, and the more you trust your own judgment, the more you'll be able to trust others as well. Let's take a look at how this concept applies to love. Why should you even try to have a new relationship if you're not willing to trust this new person 100 percent? My policy is I trust you 100 percent until you prove me wrong. And even if you disappoint me on some of my

179

How to Live a More Reckless Life

expectations, that does not make you a horrible person and my relationship with you worthless.

Nothing is ever totally "bad" or totally "good." It depends how you look at it and whether you focus on learning from it or just feeling sorry for yourself. I've seen what happens to people who feel sorry for themselves and I've decided not to follow that path. Being trusting has allowed me to fall in love more than once, to have great relationships with great men, and to not feel crestfallen when they've ended. I hope to fall in love again—for sure—before the end of my life. I have also cultivated trust in my work life, trusting that I am the right person for a given job, trusting that my ideas are meant to be realized when they're realized. Like many people, I have a whole drawer full of great un-realized ideas that I hope to someday act upon. If someone happens to act upon one of those ideas in the meantime, however, I will not be guarded or defensive or feel that life has let me down. I prefer to be open with people than guard my ideas. I prefer to convince people that I'm the right person for a job by showing my enthusiasm, energy, and passion for a project.

We live in a time when the whole concept of copyright has been transformed, and the value of an idea is actually increased by how many people can relate to that idea. I can have many more ideas and can "afford" to lose rights on some of them. I can "risk" being disappointed by a new lover, a new friend, or a new business partner because I have cultivated my fortitude—the ability not to be destroyed by mistakes, including my own. Angelika, Barbara, and I have discussed the merits of trusting, and how the benefits outweigh whatever downfalls might come about as a result. Trust is an essential virtue to being reckless.

• U IS FOR UNKNOWN •

The unknown is scary to most people. You know nothing about it and you can't use your reference system to brace yourself as you embark into the unknown. But that's also why it's so exciting! The unknown is totally new territory that you enter as an explorer, just like our ancestors ventured into totally unexplored lands. Yes, there might be unexpected dangers awaiting you. But there might also be unexpected wonderful surprises that you wouldn't get to experience if you'd just stayed home. So instead of letting fear of the unknown paralyze you, learn how to move into the new territory by taking calculated risks. How do you do that? Check out our resources section. There are many ways. One was suggested to me by "master explorer" Angelika. "Anytime I throw myself into a new challenge or expedition that would bring me to places I don't know, meeting with obstacles I cannot predict, I try to visualize how that will be, how I'd feel. It is a little bit like daydreaming. You try to be inside your visualization with all your senses alert. The unknown becomes a little more familiar and friendly that way. Then when you do physically go there, you'll be able to recognize things you've 'seen' and felt before."

• V IS FOR VARIETY •

Variety exists as a means to multiply your choices. Variety is a natural inclination of humankind. That's why we're not a carnivorous species like lions. That's why we don't have black and white vision like dogs. Humans have endless options, which can open our worldview and invite new adventures. Experience variety. Experiment with different colors, tastes, and points of view. It will make you a richer and more interesting person.

• W IS FOR WALKING •

I could have picked "wisdom," but wisdom is inherent in the cultivation of recklessness, and I've talked about it throughout the whole book. So how can walking help you find the reckless woman in you? Easy. Think about it as a meditation in movement. When you move, your mind, too, starts moving. Your mind can move away from some obstacles and blockages just by thinking about them while you're moving. Walking is not strenuous exercise. It does not require all of your attention and concentration. Plus, it can be very adventurous. It can make you discover other sides of the same streets and corners you pass by in the car every day. It can take you to places where the car cannot go. Take a walk with your lover, partner, or friend and discover how your talking acquires a different pace. Take a walk with the kids and stop often to show them flowers and trees. Let them show you the little treasures they'll find along the way, bugs included. Pay attention to little things you don't usually notice because they're just so small. And if you feel really daring, go out walking in the rain. Get wet and smell the rain in the air, the wet grass. Then enjoy a hot shower afterward. It will make you feel euphoric.

• X IS FOR XEROX •

I've always felt like Xeroxing is one of the best gifts of technology. It spares you a lot of time and handwriting, especially if yours is horrible, like mine. But a Xerox is never as beautiful or full of character as an original. Remember that in living your life. Don't mold your life as the Xerox copy of the life of your role model. Get inspired by others' pathways but find your own way. Put your heart in life and its design will soon appear in front of your eyes. Every path is good as long as it has a heart. And there are as many different paths as there are hearts.

Reckless

• Y IS FOR YOU •

There's nothing more challenging, in my opinion, than shifting the focus from yourself to others. That does not mean that you'll lose track of your identity and needs. Focus on "you" instead of "me, me, me." It will help you to avoid becoming self-centered in a culture that actually encourages self-centeredness. Paradoxically, focusing the attention away from yourself works best when you feel sad, frustrated, or depressed. "Depression comes from self-pity and self-pity comes from taking yourself too seriously," Tom Robbins once told me. I have never tried a more powerful medicine.

• Z IS FOR ZEST •

Zest is the essence of a reckless life. Zest is what you want to bring to the table when you accept a challenge or decide to follow your dreams. Zest gives your mornings a different flavor and adds a pinch of hot sauce to your nights. A bland life is as unappealing as bland food. So, since you're the chef of your life, spice it up!

Resources

BOOKS

Amazing American Women: 40 Fascinating 5-Minute Reads, by Kendall Haven (Libraries Unlimited, 1995)

Amazing Women: Amazing Firefighters, by Marsh Engle, Gay Reboli, and Anna Reboli (Jodere Group, 2002)

Dreaming with Open Eyes: The Shamanic Spirit in Twentieth Century Art and Culture, by Michael Tucker (HarperCollins, 1992)

Facing the Extreme: One Woman's Story of True Courage and Death-Defying Survival in the Eye of Mt. McKinley's Worst Storm Ever, by Ruth Anne Kocour and Michael Hodgson (St. Martin's Paperbacks, 1999)

The Future and Its Enemies: The Growing Conflict over Creativity, Enterprise, and Progress, by Virginia Postrel (Free Press, 1998)

The Gentle Tamers: Women of the Old Wild West, by Dee Brown (University of Nebraska Press, 1981)

I Shock Myself: The Autobiography of Beatrice Wood, by Beatrice Wood (Chronicle Books, 1988)

Jackie Cochran: Autobiography of the Greatest Woman Pilot In Aviation History, by Jacqueline Cochran and Maryann Bucknum Brinley (Bantam Press, 1987)

Khul-Khaal Five Egyptian Women Tell Their Stories, by Nayra Ativa (Syracuse University Press, 1982)

Lady Bullfighter: The Autobiography of the North American Matador, by Patricia McCormick (Henry Holt, 1954)

Leading Out: Mountaineering Stories of Adventurous Women by Rachel Da Silva (Seal Press, 1998)

The Legacy of Luna: The Story of a Tree, a Woman, and the Struggle to Save the Redwoods by Julia Butterfly Hill (Harper San Francisco, 2000)

Letters From India by Lady Wilson (Hippocrene Books, 1920)

The Letters of Gertrude Bell by Gertrude Bell (Penguin Travel Library, 1939)

Lucid Dreaming: A Concise Guide to Awakening in Your Dreams and in Your Life by Stephen LaBerge (Sounds True, 2004)

Mankiller: A Chief and Her People, by Wilma Mankiller and Michael Wallis (St. Martin's, 1999)

Nobody Said Not to Go: The Life, Loves, and Adventures of Emily Hahn, by Ken Cuthbertson (Faber & Faber, 1999)

Outrageous Women of Ancient Times, by Vicki León (John Wiley and Sons, 1997)

Outrageous Women of the American Frontier, by Mary Rodd Furbee (John Wiley and Sons, 2002)

Outrageous Women of Civil War Times, by Mary Rodd Furbee (John Wiley and Sons, 2003)

Race Across Alaska: First Woman to Win the Iditarod Tells Her Story, by Libby Riddles and Tim Jones (Stackpole Books, 1988)

Sally Ride: Shooting for the Stars, by Jane and Sue Hurwitz (Ballantine Books, 1989)

The Sorcerer's Crossing: A Woman's Journey, by Taisha Abelar (Penguin, 1993)

Taking on the World: A Sailor's Extraordinary Solo Race Around the Globe, by Ellen Macarthur (International Marine Publishing, 2004)

Tent in the Clouds: The First Women's Himalayan Expedition, by Monica Jackson, Arlene Blum, and Elizabeth Stark (Seal Press, 2000)

Voyager, by Jeana Yeager and Dick Rutan (Knopf, 1987)

Women and Wilderness, by Anne LaBastille (Sierra Club Books, 1987)

Women at the Helm, by Jeannine Talley (Mother Courage Press, 1990)

Women Warriors, by Teena Apeles (Seal Press, 2003)

The Women's West, by Susan Armitage and Elizabeth Jameson (University of Oklahoma Press, 1987)

BOOKS FOR YOUNG GIRLS

Extraordinary Women Journalists (grades 5-9), by Claire Price-Groff (Children's Press, 1998)

Extraordinary Women Scientists (grades 5-9), by Darlene Stille (Children's Press, 1995)

Girls Who Rocked the World: Heroines from Sacagawea to Sheryl Swoopes, by Michelle Roehm McCann, Jerry McCann (Beyond Words Publishing, 1998)

Girls Who Rocked the World 2: From Harriet Tubman to Mia Hamm, by Michelle Roehm McCann, Jerry McCann (Beyond Words Publishing, 2000)

Gutsy Girls: Young Women Who Dare, by Tina Schwager, Michele Schuerger, and Elizabeth Verdick (Free Spirit Publishing, 1999)

The Sky's The Limit: Stories of Discovery by Women and Girls, by Catherine Thimmesh (Houghton Mifflin, 2002)

MOVIES

Kill Bill (2004, 2003)
Million Dollar Baby (2004)
Calendar Girls (2003)
Under the Tuscan Sun (2003)
Divine Secrets of the Ya-Ya Sisterhood (2002)
Frida (2002)
Real Women Have Curves (2002)
Amelie (2001)
Baise-Moi (2000)
Crouching Tiger, Hidden Dragon (2000)
Erin Brockovich (2000)
Girlfight (2000)
Girl, Interrupted (2000)
Run Lola Run (1999)
Elizabeth (1998)
How Stella Got Her Groove Back (1998)
The First Wives Club (1996)
Stealing Beauty (1996)
Boys on the Side (1995)
Waiting to Exhale (1995)
Eat Drink Man Woman (1994)
La Belle Epoque (1994)
The Joy Luck Club (1993)

189

Like Water for Chocolate (1993)

A League of Their Own (1992)

Enchanted April (1991)

Fried Green Tomatoes (1991)

La Femme Nikita (1991)

Thelma and Louise (1991)

Postcards from the Edge (1990)

Shirley Valentine (1989)

Steel Magnolias (1989)

Beaches (1988)

Dirty Dancing (1987)

The Color Purple (1985)

Annie Hall (1977)

Harold and Maude (1971)

The Graduate (1967)

Two Women (1961)

Jules and Jim (1962)

The Miracle Worker (1962)

Johnny Guitar (1953)

SOURCES

www.womensrace.com/index_content.php
Adventure races where women compete in mystery events and build their own boats to race

www.distinguishedwomen.com/
Distinguished women of past and present

www.journeywoman.com
Women sharing stories of adventure

Reckless

www.thirtythousandfeet.com/women.htm
Women in aviation

www.adventurewomen.com
All-women adventure travel

www.adventuredivas.com
Stories, dispatches, tours, and advice from and for women travelers

http://sportsillustrated.cnn.com/siforwomen/top_100/1/
Sports Illustrated for Women's 100 greatest female athletes

http://heim.ifi.uio.no/~thomas/lists/amazons.html
Newsletter for and about Amazons (physically and psychologically strong, assertive women who are not afraid to break free from traditional ideas about gender roles, femininity, and the female physique) and their friends, fans, supporters, and lovers

www.gladiatrix.info
The history of female gladiators in ancient Rome

www.gonomad.com
Resource for women who travel solo or on adventures

http://Womens-travel.gordonsguide.com
Women-only adventure travel site that provides links to travel publications, destination information, and bargains

www.callwild.com
Supplies adventure trips for women with activities including kayaking and backpacking

BLOGS

www.be-reckless.com
The *Reckless* website and blog, where you can get updates on the women profiled in this book and other reckless women. Please visit and post your comments.

www.blogmechanics.com/bob/results.html
This site provides "best of" blogs divided into diverse categories with topics such as cooking, music, sex, humor, and inspiration.

http://ebonbutterfly.blogs.com/
A female artist shares her opinion on movies and art.

http://blog.barlowfriendz.net/
John Perry Barlow has been a fellow at Harvard law and a songwriter for The Greatful Dead and The String Cheese Incident. He has conversations about political topics, cyberspace, women, raising daughters, and more.

http://heathervescent.blogs.com/heathervescent/
Energetic woman named Heather shares her enthusiasm, adventures, hobbies, favorite music, and books.

www.geminica.com
Female artist talks about self-identity, art, and living in Portland, Oregon.

http://yoko.typepad.com/
Yoko is an aikido enthusiast who likes to talk about food, knitting, music, and football.

www.wildbell.com/sic.html
Journalist William Campbell shares his views (political and personal). Includes a list of "good reads" directing users to more blogs.

Acknowledgments

I appreciate this opportunity to give thanks to the many women who helped nurture this project from an idea into a book, and to a few men who made me a feminist who believes in men's goodness.

First and foremost, I owe a terrific debt of gratitude to all the women in this book, my all-star team of wild women who continue to inspire me, and many other women who were not included in this book. Thank you all for being who you are.

My very deep thanks to Franco Bolelli, my best supporter, who never thought I was using my talents to their fullest until I finally decided to pursue this book project. Thanks for pushing me to overcome my shyness and my own limits. Thank you also for our endless friendship and ever-transforming relationship that challenges every possible existing stereotype in matters of the heart.

To Daniele Bolelli, my lovely warrior son, who has been and will forever be the sunshine in my life.

To Tom Robbins, who made me love even rainy days and encouraged me to strive for a writing style that "sings in the shower and lullabies babies," and to Alexa Robbins, the wolf-eyed, wild tarot princess.

To Litty Mathew, my friend and supporter, who helped me transition from writing in my native language to—I hope—decent English.

To Zina Corace, who, at age eighty, came to America with me because she wanted a vacation "à la Thelma et Louise." You're the greatest, not only a fabulous grandmother to my son but a wise confidant and a lot of fun! You're a crazy wise woman, as Tom Robbins would say, and I had a hell of a time with you. Come again!

To Marina Mattioni, my big sister and fellow adventurer, and Claudio Mattioni, my beloved brother.

To my aunt Marilde for passing down all of Grandma's recipes and culinary secrets. I feel very privileged to be the caretaker of such a family treasure.

To James Weddell, Jim, remain who you are, keep a smile on your face, and don't ever give up. Just like the women in this book never did.

To Brooke Warner, my very honest and very patient editor at Seal Press, who endorsed this project with enthusiasm from the beginning and made it possible. I appreciate your straightforwardness and support.

And to everybody else at Seal Press who made me feel like I've finally landed on the right planet.

About the Author

✦ ✦ ✦

Gloria Mattioni was born in Milano, Italy, in 1957. She dreamed of being a pirate and an explorer and sought out people who shared similar longings. In 1988 she quit her last full-time job and pursued her goal of seeking out amazing women and incredible adventures all over the world. In 1992 she moved to Los Angeles with her son, Daniele.

Photo Credits

Libby, pages 1 and 13: © Jeff Schultz/AlaskaStock.com

Angelika and Barbara, pages 23, 27, and 33: © Robert Houser

Gevin, page 39: © Gloria Mattioni, and page 43: Courtesy of TBS

Julia Butterfly, pages 59 and 74: © Shaun Walker

Lisa, pages 81 and 91: © Gloria Mattioni

Polly, pages 99 and 111: Courtesy of Polly Matzinger

Wilma, page 121: © Gloria Mattioni

Annie, pages 145 and 156: © UltimateBet.com

Gloria, page 197: Courtesy of Gloria Mattioni

Selected Titles from Seal Press

For more than twenty-five years, Seal Press has published groundbreaking books. By women. For women. Visit our website at www.sealpress.com.

Waking up American: Coming of Age Biculturally edited by Angela Jane Fountas. $15.95, 1-58005-136-7. Twenty-two first-generation women—of Filipino, German, Mexican, Iranian, and Nicaraguan descent, among others—write about what it's like to be caught between two worlds.

The Unsavvy Traveler: Women's Comic Tales of Catastrophe edited by Rosemary Caperton, Anne Mathews, and Lucie Ocenas. $15.95, 1-58005-058-1. Thirty gut-wrenchingly funny true stories respond to the question: What happens when trips go wrong?

Above Us Only Sky by Marion Winik. $14.95, 1-58005-144-8. These witty and engaging essays from an NPR commentator address facing midlife without getting hung up on the future or tangled up in the past.

Solo: On Her Own Adventure edited by Susan Fox Rogers. $15.95, 1-58005-137-5. The second edition of this collection describes the inspiring challenges and exhilarating rewards of going it alone.

Women Who Eat: A New Generation on the Glory of Food edited by Leslie Miller. $15.95, 1-58005-092-1. More than just great food writing, this long-overdue rebuttal to the notion that all women are on a diet celebrates food with grace, wit, and gusto.

Italy, A Love Story: Women Write about the Italian Experience edited by Camille Cusumano. $15.95, 1-58005-143-X. Two dozen women describe the country they love and why they fell under its spell.